THE ULTIMATE
PHILADELPHIA EAGLES
TRIVIA BOOK

A Collection of Amazing Trivia Quizzes
and Fun Facts for Die-Hard Eagles Fans!

Ray Walker

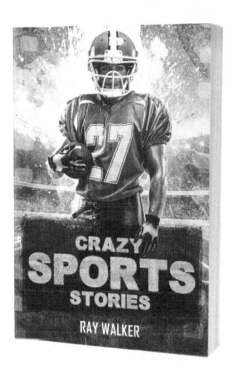

CONTENTS

INTRODUCTION

The Philadelphia Eagles were established in 1933 in Philadelphia, Pennsylvania. The Eagles have consistently proven themselves to be a team that fights hard and is a force to be reckoned with in the NFL.

The Eagles won one Super Bowl championship, in 2017. Before the Super Bowl existed, they won NFL championships in 1948, 1949, and 1960. They have also won three NFC championships and 11 NFC East division championships. They are very often a threat in the NFC East, having last won it in 2019. They have made 27 NFL playoff appearances.

Football is a lot like life. There are good times and bad times, good days and bad days, but you have to do your absolute best to never give up. The Philadelphia Eagles have proven that they refuse to give up and that they will do anything they need to do to bring a championship to the state of Pennsylvania.

Winning is more than possible when you have a storied past, as the Eagles do. They have so much captivating history and so many undeniable player legacies to be profoundly proud of. Just consider the nine players whose uniform numbers have been retired by the Eagles: Donovan McNabb, Steve Van

Buren, Brian Dawkins, Tom Brookshier, Pete Retzlaff, Chuck Bednarik, Al Wistert, Reggie White, and Jerome Brown.

The Eagles' current home is Lincoln Financial Field, which opened in 2003. They play in one of the most difficult divisions in the NFL, the NFC East, alongside the Dallas Cowboys, New York Giants, and Washington Football Team.

With such a rich past that goes back generations, you're probably already very knowledgeable as the die-hard Eagles fan that you are. Let's test that knowledge to see if you truly are the world's biggest Eagles fan.

CHAPTER 1:

ORIGINS & HISTORY

QUIZ TIME!

1. Which of the following team names did the Eagles franchise once go by?

    a. Steelers

    b. Steagles

    c. Crows

    d. Hummingbirds

2. In what year was the Philadelphia Eagles franchise established?

    a. 1925

    b. 1930

    c. 1933

    d. 1941

3. The Eagles' current home stadium is Lincoln Financial Field.

    a. True

    b. False

4. Which division do the Philadelphia Eagles play in?

   a. NFC North

   b. AFC East

   c. AFC North

   d. NFC East

5. The Philadelphia Eagles have sold out every home game since the 1999 season.

   a. True

   b. False

6. How many NFC championships have the Eagles won (as of the end of the 2020 season)?

   a. 2

   b. 3

   c. 4

   d. 7

7. What is the name of the Eagles' mascot?

   a. Glider

   b. Soar

   c. Dart

   d. Swoop

8. Who is the winningest head coach in Philadelphia Eagles history (as of the 2020 season)?

   a. Andy Reid

   b. Doug Pederson

   c. Greasy Neale

   d. Dick Vermeil

9. Who was the current head coach of the Philadelphia Eagles?

    a. Andy Reid
    b. Doug Pederson
    c. Chip Kelly
    d. Ray Rhodes

10. Who was the first head coach of the Philadelphia Eagles?

    a. Bert Bell
    b. Greasy Neale
    c. Lud Wray
    d. Jim Trimble

11. The Philadelphia Eagles have retired nine numbers.

    a. True
    b. False

12. What is the name of the Eagles' fight song?

    a. "Soar, Eagles, Soar"
    b. "The American Eagle"
    c. "Soar with the Eagles"
    d. "Fly, Eagles, Fly"

13. How many times have the Philadelphia Eagles reached the NFL playoffs (as of the end of the 2020 season)?

    a. 17
    b. 20
    c. 27
    d. 30

14. How many Super Bowl titles have the Philadelphia Eagles won (as of the end of the 2020 season)?

    a. 0
    b. 1
    c. 2
    d. 3

15. Jeffrey Lurie is the current owner of the Philadelphia Eagles.

    a. True
    b. False

16. What was the first home stadium of the Eagles franchise?

    a. Connie Mack Stadium
    b. Baker Bowl
    c. Philadelphia Municipal Stadium
    d. Veterans Stadium

17. How many NFC East division titles have the Eagles won (as of the end of the 2020 season)?

    a. 8
    b. 10
    c. 11
    d. 14

18. Before the creation of the NFC, the Eagles were in the NFL's East Division. How many East Division titles did the Philadelphia Eagles franchise win?

    a. 0
    b. 1

c. 2

d. 3

19. Carson Wentz is the current quarterback of the Philadelphia Eagles (as of the 2020 season).

   a. True

   b. False

20. The Eagles franchise was established as a replacement for the bankrupt Frankford Yellow Jackets.

   a. True

   b. False

QUIZ ANSWERS

1. B – Steagles

2. C – 1933

3. A – True

4. D – NFC East

5. A – True

6. B – 3

7. D – Swoop

8. A – Andy Reid

9. B – Doug Pederson

10. C – Lud Wray

11. A – True

12. D – "Fly, Eagles, Fly"

13. C – 27

14. B – 1

15. A – True

16. B – Baker Bowl

17. C – 11

18. D – 3

19. A – True

20. A – True

DID YOU KNOW?

1. The Eagles franchise has had 23 different head coaches so far in their history. They are Lud Wray, Bert Bell, Greasy Neale, Bo McMillin, Wayne Millner, Jim Trimble, Hugh Devore, Buck Shaw, Nick Skorich, Joe Kuharich, Jerry Williams, Ed Khayat, Mike McCormack, Dick Vermeil, Marion Campbell, Fred Bruney, Buddy Ryan, Rich Kotite, Ray Rhodes, Andy Reid, Chip Kelly, Pat Shurmur, and Doug Pederson.

2. The Eagles' current head coach is Doug Pederson. He was previously the offensive quality control coordinator and quarterbacks coach for the Eagles and offensive coordinator for the Kansas City Chiefs. During his playing career, he spent the 1999 season as an Eagle. In his second season as head coach, the Eagles won their first Super Bowl championship. He is only the fourth person to win a Super Bowl as both a player and a head coach.

3. Andy Reid is the Philadelphia Eagles' all-time winningest head coach with a 130-93-1 record.

4. The Eagles have retired nine players' numbers: Donovan McNabb (#5), Steve Van Buren (#15), Brian Dawkins (#20), Tom Brookshier (#40), Pete Retzlaff (#44), Chuck Bednarik (#60), Al Wistert (#70), Reggie White (#92), and Jerome Brown (#99).

5. Philadelphia and the Eagles have never hosted the Super Bowl.

6. The Eagles' franchise is currently headquartered at the NovaCare Complex in Philadelphia, Pennsylvania.

7. The Eagles have made three Super Bowl appearances. In those Super Bowls, they have faced the Oakland Raiders (1980) and the New England Patriots (2004, 2017).

8. The current owner of the Philadelphia Eagles is Jeffrey Lurie. He is a movie producer and businessman.

9. The Eagles' mascot Swoop is an eagle himself. He actually made a cameo in the film *Ace Ventura: Pet Detective.* During Eagles' games, Swoop can be seen zip-lining across and parachuting into the stadium.

10. The Eagles' cheerleading squad is known as the Philadelphia Eagles Cheerleaders. They were previously known as the Eaglettes and the Liberty Belles.

CHAPTER 2:

JERSEYS & NUMBERS

QUIZ TIME!

1. The original Philadelphia Eagles team colors were Kelly green, silver, and white.

    a. True
    b. False

2. What are the Eagles' current team colors?

    a. Forest green, silver, and black
    b. Forest green, silver, and white
    c. Midnight green, silver, and white
    d. Midnight green, silver, and black

3. From 1948 to 1995, the Eagles' team logo was an eagle in flight carrying a football in its claws.

    a. True
    b. False

4. What uniform number did Brian Dawkins wear as a member of the Eagles?

a. 10

b. 20

c. 30

d. 40

5. What uniform number does quarterback Carson Wentz currently wear?

   a. 9

   b. 10

   c. 11

   d. 12

6. What uniform number did Donovan McNabb wear with the Eagles?

   a. 2

   b. 3

   c. 4

   d. 5

7. As an Eagle, Jason Peters wore the uniform No. 71.

   a. True

   b. False

8. What uniform number did Harold Carmichael wear with the Eagles?

   a. 7

   b. 70

   c. 17

   d. 18

9. What uniform number did Randall Cunningham wear with the Eagles?

   a. 1
   b. 7
   c. 10
   d. 12

10. To celebrate the team's 75th anniversary, the Eagles' 2007 uniforms featured a "75 seasons" logo patch on the left shoulder.

    a. True
    b. False

11. What uniform number did Eric Allen wear as an Eagle?

    a. 2
    b. 12
    c. 21
    d. 22

12. What uniform number did Ron Jaworski wear with the Eagles?

    a. 7
    b. 16
    c. 17
    d. 21

13. In 2018, the Eagles' midnight green pants were not worn at all, marking the first time since 1996 that the Eagles wore only white pants with their white or midnight green jerseys.

    a. True
    b. False

14. What uniform number did Randy Logan wear with the Eagles?

    a. 14
    b. 41
    c. 44
    d. 49

15. What uniform number did Tra Thomas wear with the Eagles?

    a. 52
    b. 62
    c. 72
    d. 82

16. What uniform number did Jerry Sisemore wear with the Eagles?

    a. 63
    b. 66
    c. 67
    d. 76

17. What uniform number did Troy Vincent wear as an Eagle?

    a. 21
    b. 23
    c. 25
    d. 27

18. What uniform number did Steve Van Buren wear with the Eagles?

    a. 15
    b. 20

c. 25

d. 30

19. What uniform number did Tom Brookshier wear with the Eagles?

    a. 40

    b. 45

    c. 50

    d. Both A and B

20. The Eagles have retired nine uniform numbers.

    a. True

    b. False

QUIZ ANSWERS

1. A – True

2. D – Midnight green, silver, and black

3. A – True

4. B – 20

5. C – 11

6. D – 5

7. A – True

8. C – 17

9. D – 12

10. A – True

11. C – 21

12. A – 7

13. A – True

14. B – 41

15. C – 72

16. D – 76

17. B – 23

18. A – 15

19. D – Both A and B

20. A – True

DID YOU KNOW?

1. In Week 6 of the 2017 season, the Eagles debuted an all-white look with white jerseys, white pants, and solid white socks in a road game against the Carolina Panthers. The all-white look was then used full-time as a road uniform.

2. With the Eagles, Pete Retzlaff wore the Nos. 25 and 44.

3. During his time with the Eagles, Chuck Bednarik wore the No. 60.

4. Jalen Hurts currently wears No. 2 for the Philadelphia Eagles.

5. With the Eagles, Al Wistert wore No. 70.

6. In Week 6 of 2014, against the New York Giants, the Eagles introduced black pants to complement their black jerseys, giving them a blackout uniform.

7. Both the Eagles logo and uniforms were altered drastically in 1996. Kelly green was changed to "midnight green" and silver was practically abandoned, as their pants were changed to either white or midnight green. The traditional helmet wings were changed to primarily white with silver and black accents. In the logo, the eagle was changed to a white head, drawn in a less realistic, more cartoon style. Team lettering was also changed to block letters.

8. During his time with the Eagles, Jerome Brown wore No. 99.

9. DeSean Jackson currently wears No. 10 for the Philadelphia Eagles.

10. Miles Sanders currently wears No. 26 for the Philadelphia Eagles.

CHAPTER 3:

FAMOUS QUOTES

QUIZ TIME!

1. Which former Eagles player once said: "If you don't feel you're the best, then you shouldn't be doing your job. No one cares if you don't care about yourself"?

    a. Nick Foles

    b. Ron Jaworski

    c. Donovan McNabb

    d. Norm Van Brocklin

2. Which former Eagles player once said: "God places the heaviest burden on those who can carry its weight"?

    a. LeSean McCoy

    b. Eric Allen

    c. Harold Carmichael

    d. Reggie White

3. Steve Van Buren once said: "Winners, I am convinced, imagine their dreams first. They want it with all their heart and expect it to come true. There is, I believe, no other way to win."

a. True

b. False

4. Which Eagles head coach once said: "I learned a long time ago not to worry about things I can't control. Life is too short. I'm only going to focus on today"?

   a. Andy Reid

   b. Doug Pederson

   c. Chip Kelly

   d. Dick Vermeil

5. Which Eagles head coach once said: "Respecting people is an important part of life, whether it's the person doing janitorial work or the person above you. It doesn't matter who you are: I'm going to respect you"?

   a. Andy Reid

   b. Doug Pederson

   c. Chip Kelly

   d. Dick Vermeil

6. Which former Eagles player is quoted as saying: "If you align expectations with reality, you will never be disappointed"?

   a. Trent Cole

   b. Troy Vincent

   c. Terrell Owens

   d. Tra Thomas

7. Which former Eagles player is quoted as saying: "I'm always striving to do more. Whatever I accomplish, it's not enough. I don't get satisfied"?

a. Brian Westbrook

b. Brian Dawkins

c. Randall Cunningham

d. DeSean Jackson

8. Former Eagles player Norm Van Brocklin once said: "Pressure is something you feel when you don't know what the hell you're doing."

a. True

b. False

9. Which Eagles head coach once said: "If you don't invest very much, then defeat doesn't hurt very much and winning is not very exciting"?

a. Dick Vermeil

b. Andy Reid

c. Ray Rhodes

d. Buck Shaw

10. "_____, Eagles, _____!"

a. Soar

b. Win

c. Go

d. Fly

11. Which former Eagles player is quoted as saying: "You've got to play with that killer instinct, man. You've got to hate that guy across from you. Then after the game is over, tell him what a nice guy he is. Shake his hand. Especially if you win"?

a. Chuck Bednarik

b. Reggie White

c. Jerome Brown

d. Eric Allen

12. Which former Eagles player is quoted as saying: "We have the most passionate fans. You can see it in the stadium, you can see it when you're around town. It's something special"?

a. Duce Staley

b. Nick Foles

c. Donovan McNabb

d. Reggie White

13. Which Eagles player is quoted as saying: "They're passionate here. They hate losing. I'm like 'Heck I fit right in.' I hate losing. I'm real passionate about the game as well. I think that's the general consensus that I keep getting from this Philadelphia area"?

a. Jason Peters

b. Jalen Hurts

c. Carson Wentz

d. Zach Ertz

14. Which former Eagles player is quoted as saying: "I give so much of myself on Sunday. I drain all the life out of myself out there. I get paid to play, to win, to give the city pride, so maybe everybody can forget for a little while how hard life is"?

a. Randall Cunningham

b. Jeremiah Trotter

c. Harold Carmichael

d. Terrell Owens

15. Which Eagles player is quoted as saying: "Positive thinking is the key to success in business, education, pro football, anything that you can mention. I go out there thinking that I'm going to complete every pass"?

a. Sonny Jurgensen

b. Jalen Hurts

c. Donovan McNabb

d. Ron Jaworski

16. Former Eagle Eric Allen once said: "If you aren't going all the way, why go at all?"

a. True

b. False

17. Which former Eagles head coach is quoted as saying: "Everybody has the same amount of time during the day. You can either spend your time or invest your time"?

a. Buck Shaw

b. Buddy Ryan

c. Chip Kelly

d. Rich Kotite

18. Which former Eagles player is quoted as saying: "To be on the field with six, seven, eight Pro Bowlers at the same time was overwhelming. It was scary. The one thing I

realized is that they may not know you, but they respect hard work and discipline. And I was able to show that"?

a. Brian Dawkins
b. Brian Westbrook
c. LeSean McCoy
d. Seth Joyner

19. Which former Eagles player once said: "Strive to be the very best you can be. Run the race against yourself and not the guy in the other lane. The reason I say that is, as long as you give it 110%, you are going to succeed. But as long as you're trying to beat the guy over there, you are worried about him; you're not worrying about how you've got to perform"?

a. Jeremiah Trotter
b. Clyde Simmons
c. Herschel Walker
d. Mike Quick

20. Michael Vick once said: "Sometimes as a man, you fear what you can't see. Nobody can predict the future. You don't know what's going to happen. Tomorrow's not promised. The only thing you can do is live your life, hope for the best, continue to have faith, believe in yourself."

a. True
b. False

QUIZ ANSWERS

1. C – Donovan McNabb

2. D – Reggie White

3. B – False (Joe Montana said it.)

4. B – Doug Pederson

5. A – Andy Reid

6. C – Terrell Owens

7. B – Brian Dawkins

8. B – False (Peyton Manning said it.)

9. A – Dick Vermeil

10. D – Fly

11. A – Chuck Bednarik

12. B – Nick Foles

13. C – Carson Wentz

14. A – Randall Cunningham

15. D – Ron Jaworski

16. B – False (Joe Namath said it.)

17. C – Chip Kelly

18. B – Brian Westbrook

19. C – Herschel Walker

20. A – True

DID YOU KNOW?

1. "When I look back on my career, I consider myself very fortunate just to have the opportunity to play professional football. You remember I went to Duke University, I think we only threw the ball something like 53 times my senior year there. I really wasn't schooled for coming into professional football." – Sonny Jurgensen in his Pro Football Hall of Fame enshrinement speech

2. "I signed with the Philadelphia Eagles in 1964 where Joe Kuharich was not only my head coach but he was also like a second father to me, a man I respected and I loved. My line coach in Philadelphia was Dick Stanfel, who was also been nominated to this Hall of Fame and I hope one day he will be enshrined. Coach Stanfel was an All-Pro guard for the Detroit Lions and an absolute genius tactician of line play. He encouraged my super aggressive Def Con 5 style and he helped me to develop my unorthodox line stance. As a rookie, I brought to the Eagles desire to win, the need to be the best, an uncompromising work ethic to accomplish both. Coach Stanfel taught me how to take the talents that I brought to the Eagles and forged it into a workable tool that ultimately placed me here today." – Bob "Boomer" Brown in his Pro Football Hall of Fame enshrinement speech

3. "I want to thank the organizations, especially the Chicago Bears, the Philadelphia Eagles, and Dallas Cowboys for

making my 27 years in football something special. I want to thank the NFL for what it stands for, for the men who played the game for what it really is." – Mike Ditka in his Pro Football Hall of Fame enshrinement speech

4. "I want to thank coach Greasy Neale for having the guts and temerity for picking me as a lineman as his first pick in giving me the opportunity and being my first coach in professional football. I want to thank my parents for bringing me up to be a good strong, healthy boy. I want to thank my wife, who put up with me for these fourteen years and raised my five daughters for me while I was out gallivanting on football fields." – Chuck Bednarik in his Pro Football Hall of Fame enshrinement speech

5. "We're talking about history. We knew Reggie, Reggie's history in football. Just like Jeremy said, Reggie's legacy will live on through you. If you continue to do what you need to do, and your family first, your community, your school, at your work, job, your legacy, you would take Reggie's spirit and legacy with you because that's what he would want you to do. One last thing is that, remember, it's not how you die, it wasn't about Reggie's death, it's how he lived. I encourage you to live like Reggie lived. Thank you so much." – Sara White on behalf of the late Reggie White at his Pro Football Hall of Fame enshrinement

6. "And, finally, let's talk about these Eagles fans. I read—I know some of you drove all the way from Philly here. And, listen, I have a good understanding that you don't have money just to waste. So that means that you put

hard-earned money that you could be saving to come out here and celebrate with your boy!

7. "So, thank you! Thank you for loving me the way that I love you. I love you back. And I thank you. Thank you for everything." – Brian Dawkins in his Pro Football Hall of Fame enshrinement speech

8. "Thank you, thank you, thank you. You know, I grew up in a time where a man always said, I have a dream, and that man was Martin Luther King. And as a kid growing up at that time, listening to him, all I could do is dream. I wanted to be someone special that my mother and my father and my family looked up to. I wanted to be someone that, you know, I enjoyed playing a game, but then again I enjoyed working and just trying to take care of myself." – Richard Dent in his Pro Football Hall of Fame enshrinement speech

9. "But from the time I first picked up a football I fell in love with this game. It's all I ever wanted to do. From playing tackle in the streets of White Plains to playing in the stadiums in the NFL, I never ever imagined it would take me this far. It's taken a lot of hard work and sacrifice and the belief from people and times when I didn't believe in myself. I've experienced some exciting moments. I've met some extraordinary people and I have a lot of great memories that I will never forget.

10. "This is the icing on the cake for me, and I take it very seriously. And I'm extremely honored to now be included with this group of elite athletes and to do so with my Class

of 2008. I will wear the banner with pride. And I will represent it well." – Art Monk in his Pro Football Hall of Fame enshrinement speech

11. "My teammates from Philadelphia where I was drafted, the Philadelphia Eagles organization, they took a chance on me. Buddy Ryan drafted me, and he tried to grow me up in the league. What Buddy Ryan did was the best thing that ever happened for me when he cut me and told me I couldn't play for his football team. But he told me a story. He told me the night before he went on and talked to his wife, and he asked his wife what he should do. And his wife told him, don't cut Cris Carter. He's going to do something special with his life. So Buddy Ryan, and your lovely wife, I thank you. You're going into the hall with me tonight.

12. "And the fifth person I met was the Minister of Defense, and his name was Reggie White. I grew up in a single-parent home. Reggie White, when I was 22, was the first man to tell me he loved me. And he said, 'Cris, through God all things are possible.' Now, there might be a lot of people you might question where they're at, but I know, Big Dog. I know you looking down, and I know you're happy with me. I appreciate you, Reggie. I love you." – Cris Carter in his Pro Football Hall of Fame enshrinement speech

13. "Then came the Philadelphia Eagles. I got traded to the Eagles. I met a man that had better work ethics than I did. I marveled at the way he went about his job. His name is

Coach Dick Vermeil. Dick, would you stand? Let the people see you. This man worked tirelessly to take a football team that perhaps may not have been a great football team, but he had a bunch of young guys who really got into what he was preaching, and we ended up going to a Super Bowl. Coach Vermeil and I are still good friends. We talk occasionally. Coach and his wife Carol ended up being just great friends to me. I appreciate Coach.

14. "When I got to Philadelphia, man, what a nice young team. Those guys accepted me. They brought me in. They were like sponges. They wanted to know what it was that I had been doing to get to All-Pro or make All-Pro." – Claude Humphrey in his Pro Football Hall of Fame enshrinement speech

CHAPTER 4:

CATCHY NICKNAMES

QUIZ TIME!

1. What was Chuck Bednarik's nickname?

   a. Calm Chuck

   b. Crazy Charlie

   c. Concrete Charlie

   d. Cool Chuck

2. Jerimiah Trotter went by the nickname "Axe Man."

   a. True

   b. False

3. What nickname did Ron Jaworski go by?

   a. Barracuda

   b. Ski

   c. Shark

   d. Jaws

4. What nickname does LeSean McCoy go by?

   a. Slim

   b. Shady

c. Coy

d. Sir

5. Which is NOT a nickname for the Eagles as a team?

    a. The Birds

    b. The Iggles

    c. America's Birds

    d. Gang Green

6. What nickname did Freddie Mitchell go by?

    a. Stitches

    b. Ready Freddie

    c. Steady Freddie

    d. FredEx

7. Jalen Mills was given the nickname "Green Goblin" due to coloring his hair green.

    a. True

    b. False

8. What nickname did Pete Retzlaff go by?

    a. Stinky Pete

    b. Baron

    c. Runnin' Retz

    d. None of the above

9. What nickname did Jason Peters go by?

    a. Mythical Creature

    b. Godfather

    c. The Bodyguard

    d. All of the above

10. What nickname does Terrell Owens go by?

    a. Tearin' Terrell
    b. T.O.
    c. Beast
    d. Open Owens

11. What nickname did Marion Campbell go by?

    a. Marion the Move
    b. Lake Wolf
    c. Swamp Fox
    d. Campbell's Soup

12. Jevon Kearse went by the nickname "The Freak."

    a. True
    b. False

13. What nickname did Sam Bradford go by?

    a. Ford Mustang
    b. Sammy Sleeves
    c. Sourdough Sam
    d. Brad Man

14. What nickname did Randall Cunningham go by?

    a. The Ultimate Weapon
    b. Starship 12
    c. Hammy
    d. Both A and B

15. Allegiant Stadium is nicknamed "The Linc" by Philly locals.

a. True

b. False

16. "Tra" is a nickname. What is Tra Thomas's full name?

   a. Travis Thomas III

   b. Michael Thomas III

   c. William Thomas III

   d. Matthew Thomas III

17. Current Eagle Carson Wentz goes by the nickname "Ginger Jesus."

   a. True

   b. False

18. "J.J." is a nickname. What is J.J. Arcega-Whiteside's full name?

   a. Joaquin Jose Arcega-Whiteside

   b. Jose Joaquin Arcega-Whiteside

   c. Jacob Joseph Arcega-Whiteside

   d. Joseph Jacob Arcega-Whiteside

19. What nickname does Andy Reid go by?

   a. Burger Andy

   b. Red Reid

   c. Walter Reid

   d. Big Red

20. Ricky Watters had the nicknames "Running Watters" and "Thunder."

   a. True

   b. False

QUIZ ANSWERS

1. C – Concrete Charlie

2. A – True

3. D – Jaws

4. B – Shady

5. C – America's Birds

6. D – FredEx

7. A – True

8. B – Baron

9. D – All of the above

10. B   T.O.

11. C – Swamp Fox

12. A – True

13. B – Sammy Sleeves

14. D – Both A and B

15. A – True

16. C – William Thomas III

17. A – True

18. B – Jose Joaquin Arcega-Whiteside

19. D – Big Red

20. A – True

DID YOU KNOW?

1. Former Eagle Fred Barnett went by the nickname "Arkansas Fred."

2. Former Eagle Michael Vick had the nickname "Ookie."

3. Former Eagle Nick Foles goes by the nickname "St. Nick."

4. Former Eagle Ben Hawkins was called "The Hawk."

5. Former Eagle Jim McMahon went by the nicknames "Mad Mac," "Jersey Jim," "The Punky QB," and "McManiac."

6. Former Eagle Mark Sanchez had the nickname "The Sanchize."

7. Former Eagle Norm Van Brocklin went by the nickname "The Dutchman."

8. Former Eagle Ty Detmer went by the nickname "Chicken Legs."

9. Former Eagle Darren Sproles goes by the nickname "Lightning Bug."

10. Current Eagle Miles Sanders goes by the nickname "Boobie."

CHAPTER 5:

THE MINISTER OF DEFENSE

QUIZ TIME!

1. What was Reggie White's full name?

    a. Reginald Christopher White
    b. Christopher Reginald White
    c. Reginald Howard White
    d. Howard Reginald White

2. Reggie White played his entire NFL career with the Eagles.

    a. True
    b. False

3. Where was Reggie White born?

    a. Cornelius, North Carolina
    b. Chattanooga, Tennessee
    c. Carmel, California
    d. Calhoun, Georgia

4. When was Reggie White born?

    a. December 26, 1961
    b. December 26, 1969

c. December 19, 1969

d. December 19, 1961

5. Reggie White was an ordained evangelical minister.

    a. True

    b. False

6. How many Pro Bowls was Reggie White named to in his career?

    a. 5

    b. 10

    c. 13

    d. 15

7. Where did Reggie White go to college?

    a. University of Southern California

    b. University of Tennessee

    c. University of Michigan

    d. University of Notre Dame

8. Reggie White is a member of both the College Football Hall of Fame and the Pro Football Hall of Fame.

    a. True

    b. False

9. Reggie White's No. _____ is retired by the Philadelphia Eagles, Green Bay Packers, and Tennessee Volunteers.

    a. 82

    b. 89

    c. 92

    d. 99

10. How many Super Bowls did Reggie White win in his career?

    a. 0
    b. 1
    c. 2
    d. 3

11. How many times was Reggie White named the NFL Defensive Player of the Year?

    a. 0
    b. 1
    c. 2
    d. 3

12. Reggie White's mother, Thelma Collier, told *Sports Illustrated* that, when he was 12 years old, he said that he wanted to be two things in life: a football player and a minister.

    a. True
    b. False

13. How many times was Reggie White named the NFC Defensive Player of the Year?

    a. 1
    b. 2
    c. 3
    d. 4

14. In 1997, Reggie White took part in a professional wrestling match.

a. True

b. False

15. What year was Reggie White inducted into the Pro Football Hall of Fame?

    a. 2003

    b. 2004

    c. 2005

    d. 2006

16. How many times was Reggie White named a First-Team All-Pro?

    a. 4

    b. 8

    c. 9

    d. 10

17. Reggie White Way in Green Bay, Wisconsin, is off Lombardi Avenue near Lambeau Field.

    a. True

    b. False

18. How many times in his career was Reggie White the NFL sacks leader?

    a. 1

    b. 2

    c. 3

    d. 4

19. How many times was Reggie White named a Second-Team All-Pro in his career?

a. 1

b. 2

c. 5

d. 6

20. Reggie White was named the SEC Player of the Year in 1983.

a. True

b. False

QUIZ ANSWERS

1. C – Reginald Howard White

2. B – False (He played for the Eagles, Green Bay Packers, and Carolina Panthers.)

3. B – Chattanooga, Tennessee

4. D – December 19, 1961

5. A – True

6. C – 13

7. B – University of Tennessee

8. A – True

9. C – 92

10. B – 1

11. C – 2 (1987, 1998)

12. A – True

13. C – 3 (1987, 1991, 1995)

14. A – True

15. D – 2006

16. B – 8

17. A – True

18. B – 2 (1987, 1988)

19. C – 5

20. A – True

DID YOU KNOW?

1. Reggie White passed away in 2004 due to cardiac arrhythmia and sleep apnea, plus cardiac and pulmonary sarcoidosis. White's widow, Sara, founded the Reggie White Sleep Disorders Research and Education Foundation following his death.

2. In 1996, Reggie White starred in the Christian film *Reggie's Prayer*. The film also stars Brett Favre, Mike Holmgren, and M.C. Hammer.

3. Reggie White won a Bart Starr Award in 1992.

4. White finished his NFL career with 198 sacks.

5. He was named a unanimous All-American and First-Team All-SEC in 1983.

6. Reggie White was named to both the NFL 75th Anniversary All-Time Team and the NFL 100th Anniversary All-Time Team.

7. In college, White was named the number one recruit in Tennessee by the *Knoxville News Sentinel*.

8. Reggie White did not begin his professional football career in the NFL. After his college football career, White was chosen by the Memphis Showboats in the 1984 USFL Territorial draft. When the USFL collapsed, White signed with the Eagles.

9. During the 2005 season, the Philadelphia Eagles, the Green Bay Packers, and the University of Tennessee retired Reggie White's No. 92 jersey. His jersey number retirements and Pro Football Hall of Fame induction came posthumously.

10. Reggie White was inducted into the Wisconsin Athletic Hall of Fame in 2005 and the Philadelphia Sports Hall of Fame in 2007.

CHAPTER 6:

STATISTICALLY SPEAKING

QUIZ TIME!

1. Harold Carmichael holds the Philadelphia Eagles franchise record for career receiving touchdowns with how many?

    a. 71
    b. 79
    c. 89
    d. 91

2. Terrell Owens holds the Philadelphia Eagles franchise record for receiving touchdowns in a season with 14 in 2004.

    a. True
    b. False

3. Steve Van Buren holds the franchise record for career rushing touchdowns with how many?

    a. 69
    b. 79

c. 89

d. 99

4. Zach Ertz holds Philadelphia's single-game record for the most receptions with _____ on November 11, 2018, against the Dallas Cowboys.

   a. 11

   b. 12

   c. 13

   d. 14

5. Which player holds the Philadelphia Eagles record for most sacks in a single season with 21 in 1987?

   a. Clyde Simmons

   b. Seth Joyner

   c. Reggie White

   d. Jerome Brown

6. Who holds the franchise's single-season record for most pass completions with 388?

   a. Sam Bradford

   b. Mark Sanchez

   c. Donovan McNabb

   d. Carson Wentz

7. Donovan McNabb holds the Eagle record for most career pass completions with 2,801.

   a. True

   b. False

8. LeSean McCoy holds the franchise record for most rushing touchdowns in a single season (2011) with how many?

    a. 15
    b. 16
    c. 17
    d. 18

9. Mike Quick holds the Philadelphia Eagles franchise record for most receiving yards in a single season with 1,409 in _____.

    a. 1982
    b. 1983
    c. 1984
    d. 1985

10. Who holds the franchise record with 32,837 career passing yards?

    a. Randall Cunningham
    b. Nick Foles
    c. Carson Wentz
    d. Donovan McNabb

11. Carson Wentz holds the franchise record for most passing touchdowns in a single season, with how many in 2017?

    a. 31
    b. 33
    c. 35
    d. 37

12. Sonny Jurgensen holds the Philadelphia Eagles franchise record for most passes intercepted in a single season with 26 in 1962.

    a. True
    b. False

13. Which player holds the Philadelphia Eagles franchise record for career interceptions with 34?

    a. Bill Bradley
    b. Brian Dawkins
    c. Eric Allen
    d. All of the above

14. Harold Carmichael holds the Philadelphia Eagles franchise record for most career receptions with how many?

    a. 569
    b. 579
    c. 589
    d. 599

15. Timmy Brown holds the Philadelphia Eagles franchise record for career return yards with how many?

    a. 4,887
    b. 4,997
    c. 5,007
    d. 5,500

16. Donovan McNabb holds the franchise record for most career pass attempts in the playoffs with how many?

a. 557

b. 567

c. 577

d. 587

17. Brian Westbrook holds the Philadelphia Eagles franchise record for most career games with 3 or more touchdowns scored, with seven games.

   a. True

   b. False

18. Reggie White holds the Philadelphia Eagles franchise record for most career sacks with how many?

   a. 94

   b. 104

   c. 114

   d. 124

19. Who holds the franchise record for most career games with 1+ touchdown scored with 69 games?

   a. Duce Staley

   b. Harold Carmichael

   c. LeSean McCoy

   d. Brian Westbrook

20. Wilbert Montgomery holds the Philadelphia Eagles franchise record for most 100+ yard rushing games with 26.

   a. True

   b. False

QUIZ ANSWERS

1. B – 79

2. A – True

3. A – 69

4. D – 14

5. C – Reggie White

6. D – Carson Wentz (2019)

7. A – True

8. C – 17

9. B – 1983

10. D – Donovan McNabb

11. B – 33

12. A – True

13. D – All of the above (three-way tie)

14. C – 589

15. B – 4,997

16. C – 577

17. A – True

18. D – 124

19. B – Harold Carmichael

20. A – True

DID YOU KNOW?

1. Donovan McNabb holds the Philadelphia Eagles record with 216 career passing touchdowns.

2. Wally Henry holds the Philadelphia Eagles franchise record for career punt returns with 148.

3. Allen Rossum holds the Philadelphia Eagles franchise record for kick returns in a single season with 54 in 1999.

4. Andy Reid holds the Philadelphia Eagles franchise record for most head coaching wins, with 130.

5. LeSean McCoy holds the franchise record for career rushing yards, with 6,792 yards. McCoy also holds the Eagles' single-season record for rushing yards with 1,607 in 2013.

6. Reggie White, Derrick Burgess, Hugh Douglas, and Carl Hairston are all tied for the Philadelphia Eagles franchise record for career NFL playoff sacks, with 4 each.

7. Timmy Brown holds the franchise record with 4,483 career kick return yards.

8. Brian Mitchell holds the Philadelphia Eagles franchise record for career punt return yards with 1,369 yards. Mitchell also holds the Eagles' record for punt return yards in a single season with 567 yards in 2002.

9. Randall Cunningham holds the Eagles record for being sacked with 422.

10. Ricky Watters holds the franchise record for rushing yards per game with 79 yards.

CHAPTER 7:

THE TRADE MARKET

QUIZ TIME!

1. On April 25, 2020, the Philadelphia Eagles traded a 2020 6th-round draft pick (Charlie Woerner) to the _____ in exchange for Marquise Goodwin and a 2020 6th-round draft pick (Prince Tega Wanogho).

   a. Buffalo Bills
   b. San Francisco 49ers
   c. Green Bay Packers
   d. Indianapolis Colts

2. On March 13, 2019, the Philadelphia Eagles traded Michael Bennett and a 2020 7th-round draft pick (Jashon Cornell) to the _____ in exchange for a 2020 5th-round draft pick (John Hightower).

   a. Tampa Bay Buccaneers
   b. Seattle Seahawks
   c. Dallas Cowboys
   d. New England Patriots

3. On March 14, 2018, the Philadelphia Eagles traded Torrey Smith to the Carolina Panthers in exchange for Daryl Worley.

   a. True

   b. False

4. On October 30, 2018, the Philadelphia Eagles traded a 2019 3rd-round draft pick (Cody Barton) to the Detroit Lions in exchange for _____.

   a. Zach Ertz

   b. Golden Tate

   c. Josh Adams

   d. Darren Sproles

5. On March 10, 2015, the Philadelphia Eagles traded LeSean McCoy to the Buffalo Bills in exchange for Kiko Alonso.

   a. True

   b. False

6. On March 13, 2014, the Philadelphia Eagles traded a 2014 5th-round draft pick (Ronald Powell) to the New Orleans Saints in exchange for _____.

   a. Nick Foles

   b. Jordan Matthews

   c. Darren Sproles

   d. Zach Ertz

7. On April 11, 2013, the Philadelphia Eagles traded Dion Lewis to the _____ in exchange for Emmanuel Acho.

a. Cleveland Browns

b. New England Patriots

c. Tennessee Titans

d. New York Giants

8. On April 5, 2010, the Philadelphia Eagles traded _____ to the Washington Redskins for a 2010 2nd-round draft pick (Nate Allen) and a 2010 4th-round draft pick (Alterraun Verner).

a. Michael Vick

b. DeSean Jackson

c. Reggie Brown

d. Donovan McNabb

9. On April 20, 2009, the Philadelphia Eagles traded a 2009 1st-round draft pick (Eric Wood) and a 2009 4th-round draft pick (Shawn Nelson) to the _____ in exchange for Jason Peters.

a. Buffalo Bills

b. Detroit Lions

c. Jacksonville Jaguars

d. Chicago Bears

10. On June 6, 2008, the Philadelphia Eagles traded an undisclosed 2008 draft pick to the Oakland Raiders in exchange for Luke Lawton.

a. True

b. False

11. On April 30, 2006, the Philadelphia Eagles traded Hollis Thomas and a 2006 4th-round draft pick (Jahri Evans) to the _____ for a 2006 4th-round draft pick (Max-Jean Gilles).

    a. Green Bay Packers
    b. Carolina Panthers
    c. New Orleans Saints
    d. St. Louis Rams

12. On May 18, 2006, the Philadelphia Eagles traded Billy McMullen to the Minnesota Vikings in exchange for Hank Baskett.

    a. True
    b. False

13. On April 28, 1999, the Philadelphia Eagles traded _____ to the Washington Redskins for a 2000 6th-round draft pick (John Romero).

    a. Bobby Hoying
    b. Rodney Peete
    c. Duce Staley
    d. Brian Dawkins

14. On March 16, 2004, Terrell Owens was traded to the Eagles in a three-team trade.

    a. True
    b. False

15. On August 24, 1999, the Philadelphia Eagles traded Bobby Hoying to the _____ in exchange for a 2000 6th-round draft pick (John Frank).

a. Arizona Cardinals

b. San Diego Chargers

c. Pittsburgh Steelers

d. Oakland Raiders

16. On April 19, 1997, the Philadelphia Eagles traded a 1997 3rd-round draft pick (Ty Howard) and a 1997 6th-round pick (Tony McCombs) to the Arizona Cardinals in exchange for a 1997 3rd-round draft pick (_____).

    a. Ty Detmer

    b. Ricky Watters

    c. Kevin Turner

    d. Duce Staley

17. On April 22, 1995, the Philadelphia Eagles traded a 1995 1st-round pick (Warren Sapp), 1995 2nd-round pick (Melvin Johnson), and a 1995 2nd-round draft pick (Shane Hannah) to the _____ in exchange for a 1995 1st-round draft pick (Mike Mamula) and a 1995 3rd-round draft pick (Greg Jefferson).

    a. Kansas City Chiefs

    b. Oakland Raiders

    c. Tampa Bay Buccaneers

    d. Denver Broncos

18. On August 30, 2003, the Philadelphia Eagles traded Freddie Milons to the _____ in exchange for an undisclosed 2004 draft pick.

    a. Houston Texans

    b. Atlanta Falcons

c. Seattle Seahawks

d. Pittsburgh Steelers

19. On March 3, 2004, the Philadelphia Eagles traded A.J. Feeley to the _____ in exchange for a 2005 2nd-round draft pick (Reggie Brown).

a. St. Louis Rams

b. Miami Dolphins

c. Jacksonville Jaguars

d. Atlanta Falcons

20. The Philadelphia Eagles did not make a trade in 1996 or 2002.

a. True

b. False

QUIZ ANSWERS

1. B – San Francisco 49ers

2. D – New England Patriots

3. A – True

4. B – Golden Tate

5. A – True

6. C – Darren Sproles

7. A – Cleveland Browns

8. D – Donovan McNabb

9. A – Buffalo Bills

10. B – False (The draft pick was traded to the Indianapolis Colts.)

11. C – New Orleans Saints

12. A – True

13. B – Rodney Peete

14. A – True

15. D – Oakland Raiders

16. D – Duce Staley

17. C – Tampa Bay Buccaneers

18. D – Pittsburgh Steelers

19. B – Miami Dolphins

20. A – True

DID YOU KNOW?

1. On April 26, 2009, the Philadelphia Eagles traded a 2009 5th-round draft pick (Thomas Morstead) to the New Orleans Saints for a 2009 7th-round draft pick (Pat McAfee) and a 2010 5th-round draft pick (Reshad Jones).

2. On October 20, 2009, the Philadelphia Eagles traded Brandon Gibson and a 2009 3rd-round draft pick to the St. Louis Rams in exchange for Will Witherspoon.

3. On March 17, 2010, the Philadelphia Eagles traded Chris Clemons and a 2010 4th-round draft pick (E.J. Wilson) to the Seattle Seahawks in exchange for Darryl Tapp.

4. On September 4, 2015, the Philadelphia Eagles traded Matt Barkley to the Arizona Cardinals in exchange for a 2016 7th-round draft pick (Joe Walker).

5. On September 3, 2016, the Philadelphia Eagles traded Sam Bradford to the Minnesota Vikings in exchange for a 2017 1st-round pick (Derek Barnett) and a 2018 4th-round draft pick (Josh Sweat).

6. On August 22, 2017, the Philadelphia Eagles traded Matt Tobin and a 2018 7th-round draft pick (Ryan Izzo) to the Seattle Seahawks in exchange for a 2018 5th-round draft pick (Troy Fumagalli).

7. On August 27, 2017, the Philadelphia Eagles traded Terrence Brooks to the New York Jets in exchange for Dexter McDougle.

8. On April 29, 2017, the Philadelphia Eagles traded a 2017 4th-round draft pick (Jehu Chesson) and a 2017 7th-round draft pick (Josh Harvey-Clemons) to the Minnesota Vikings for a 2017 4th-round draft pick (Donnel Pumphrey).

9. On August 22, 2019, the Philadelphia Eagles traded Bruce Hector to the Arizona Cardinals in exchange for Rudy Ford.

10. On October 28, 2019, the Philadelphia Eagles traded a 2021 4th-round draft pick to the Cleveland Browns in exchange for Genard Avery.

CHAPTER 8:

DRAFT DAY

QUIZ TIME!

1. With the 161st overall pick in the 7th round of the _____ NFL draft, the Philadelphia Eagles selected Harold Carmichael.

    a. 1970
    b. 1971
    c. 1972
    d. 1973

2. With the _____ overall pick in the 1st round of the 2016 NFL draft, the Philadelphia Eagles selected Carson Wentz.

    a. 1st
    b. 2nd
    c. 3rd
    d. 4th

3. With the 53rd overall pick in the 2nd round of the _____ NFL draft, the Philadelphia Eagles selected Jalen Hurts.

    a. 2017
    b. 2018

c. 2019

d. 2020

4. With the 37th overall pick in the 2nd round of the _____ NFL draft, the Philadelphia Eagles selected Randall Cunningham.

   a. 1983
   b. 1984
   c. 1985
   d. 1986

5. With the 30th overall pick in the 2nd round of the _____ NFL draft, the Philadelphia Eagles selected Eric Allen.

   a. 1987
   b. 1988
   c. 1989
   d. 1990

6. With the 37th overall pick in the 2nd round of the 1973 NFL draft, the _____ selected Ron Jaworski.

   a. Philadelphia Eagles
   b. Kansas City Chiefs
   c. Miami Dolphins
   d. Los Angeles Rams

7. With the 55th overall pick in the 3rd round of the 1973 NFL draft, the Philadelphia Eagles selected Randy Logan.

   a. True
   b. False

8. With the _____ overall pick in the 1st round of the 1998 NFL draft, the Philadelphia Eagles selected Tra Thomas.

    a. 1st
    b. 2nd
    c. 11th
    d. 14th

9. With the _____ overall pick in the 1st round of the 1973 NFL draft, the Philadelphia Eagles selected Jerry Sisemore.

    a. 1st
    b. 3rd
    c. 10th
    d. 13th

10. The Philadelphia Eagles drafted DeSean Jackson in the 2nd round, 49th overall in the 2008 NFL draft.

    a. True
    b. False

11. With the 7th overall pick in the 1st round of the 1992 NFL draft, the _____ selected Troy Vincent.

    a. Philadelphia Eagles
    b. Buffalo Bills
    c. Miami Dolphins
    d. Washington Redskins

12. Tom Brookshier was drafted in the 10th round, 118th overall, of the 1953 NFL draft by the Philadelphia Eagles.

    a. True
    b. False

13. With the _____ overall pick in the 1st round of the 1944 NFL draft, the Philadelphia Eagles selected Steve Van Buren.

    a. 1st
    b. 2nd
    c. 3rd
    d. 5th

14. With the 266th overall pick in the 22nd round of the 1953 NFL draft, the _____ selected Pete Retzlaff.

    a. Philadelphia Eagles
    b. New York Giants
    c. Detroit Lions
    d. San Francisco 49ers

15. With the ____ overall pick in the 1st round of the 1949 NFL draft, the Philadelphia Eagles selected Chuck Bednarik.

    a. 1st
    b. 2nd
    c. 3rd
    d. 4th

16. With the 9th overall pick in the 1st round of the _____ NFL draft, the Philadelphia Eagles selected Jerome Brown.

    a. 1986
    b. 1987
    c. 1988
    d. 1989

17. With the 1st overall pick in the 1st round of the 2001 NFL draft, the _____ selected Michael Vick.

    a. Philadelphia Eagles

    b. New York Jets

    c. Pittsburgh Steelers

    d. Atlanta Falcons

18. Ricky Watters was drafted in the 2nd round, 45th overall in the 1991 NFL draft by the _____.

    a. Philadelphia Eagles

    b. Seattle Seahawks

    c. San Francisco 49ers

    d. Los Angeles Raiders

19. Terrell Owens was drafted in the 3rd round, 89th overall in the 1996 NFL draft by the _____.

    a. Philadelphia Eagles

    b. Dallas Cowboys

    c. San Francisco 49ers

    d. Cincinnati Bengals

20. Al Wistert was selected by the Phil-Pitt Steagles in the 5th round, 32nd overall in the 1943 NFL draft.

    a. True

    b. False

QUIZ ANSWERS

1. B – 1971

2. B – 2nd

3. D – 2020

4. C – 1985

5. B – 1988

6. D – Los Angeles Rams

7. A – True

8. C – 11th

9. B – 3rd

10. A – True

11. C – Miami Dolphins

12. A – True

13. D – 5th

14. C – Detroit Lions

15. A – 1st

16. B – 1987

17. D – Atlanta Falcons

18. C – San Francisco 49ers

19. C – San Francisco 49ers

20. A – True

DID YOU KNOW?

1. Former Eagle LeSean McCoy was selected by the Philadelphia Eagles in the 2nd round, 53rd overall in the 2009 NFL draft.

2. Former Eagle William Thomas was selected by the Philadelphia Eagles in the 4th round, 104th overall in the 1991 NFL draft.

3. Former Eagle Jim McMahon was selected by the Chicago Bears in the 1st round, 5th overall in the 1982 NFL draft.

4. Former Eagle Herschel Walker was selected by the Dallas Cowboys in the 5th round, 114th overall in the 1985 NFL draft.

5. Former Eagle Rodney Peete was selected by the Detroit Lions in the 6th round, 141st overall in the 1989 NFL draft.

6. Current Eagle Zach Ertz was selected by the Philadelphia Eagles in the 2nd round, 35th overall in the 2013 NFL draft.

7. Former Eagle Bill Bergey was selected by the Cincinnati Bengals in the 2nd round, 31st overall in the 1969 NFL draft.

8. Former Eagle Nick Foles was selected by the Philadelphia Eagles in the 3rd round, 88th overall in the 2012 NFL draft.

9. Former Eagle Brian Westbrook was selected by the Philadelphia Eagles in the 3rd round, 91st overall in the 2002 NFL draft.

10. Former Eagle Sonny Jurgensen was selected by the Philadelphia Eagles in the 4th round, 43rd overall in the 1957 NFL draft.

CHAPTER 9:

ODDS & ENDS

QUIZ TIME!

1. Which former Eagles player appeared on *The Celebrity Apprentice*?

    a. Reggie White
    b. Donovan McNabb
    c. Terrell Owens
    d. Michael Vick

2. Brian Westbrook is the cousin of the NBA's Russell Westbrook.

    a. True
    b. False

3. Former Eagle Jon Dorenbos appeared on _____, showcasing his magic tricks.

    a. Fear Factor
    b. Shark Tank
    c. Britain's Got Talent
    d. America's Got Talent

4. In March 2013, Randall Cunningham's book was published. What is its title?

    a. Cunningham
    b. Lay It Down: How Letting Go Brings Out Your Best
    c. My Life: Randall Cunningham
    d. The Quarterback

5. Following high school graduation, Chuck Bednarik entered the _____.

    a. United States Marine Corps
    b. United States Navy
    c. United States Army Air Forces
    d. United States Coast Guard

6. Who is currently the Executive Vice President of Football Operations for the NFL?

    a. Troy Vincent
    b. Seth Joyner
    c. David Akers
    d. Jerome Brown

7. Eric Allen is the brother of former NFL player Marcus Allen.

    a. True
    b. False

8. Who was featured on the cover of the PlayStation 2 version of NCAA Football '09?

    a. Carson Wentz
    b. Brian Dawkins

    c. LeSean McCoy

    d. DeSean Jackson

9. Which famous NBA star is a fan of the Philadelphia Eagles?

    a. Kobe Bryant

    b. Steph Curry

    c. LeBron James

    d. Shaquille O'Neal

10. Terrell Owens is the only inductee of the Pro Football Hall of Fame to skip his induction ceremony and instead host a separate induction ceremony.

    a. True

    b. False

11. Which of the following businesses does Jeremiah Trotter own?

    a. Car wash

    b. Salon

    c. Restaurant

    d. Both A and B

12. Tra Thomas is the brother of MLB legend Frank Thomas.

    a. True

    b. False

13. Michael Vick spent 21 months in federal prison for his involvement in what?

    a. Burglary

    b. Dog fighting

c. Drunk driving

d. Embezzlement

14. In 2018, Nick Foles released an autobiography entitled
_____.

    a. In the Nick of Time

    b. Foles

    c. Believe It: My Journey of Success, Failure, and Overcoming the Odds

    d. Believe in Yourself: The Nick Foles Story

15. Former Eagle turned actor Nnamdi Asomugha is married to which actress?

    a. Halle Berry

    b. Kerry Washington

    c. Tamera Mowry

    d. Gabrielle Union

16. Jon Runyan was the U.S. Representative for New Jersey's 3rd congressional district from 2011 to 2015.

    a. True

    b. False

17. Carson Wentz is a friend of which MLB star?

    a. Clayton Kershaw

    b. Bryce Harper

    c. Aaron Judge

    d. Mike Trout

18. The "Duce Staley Drill," a practice drill that Staley created to enhance players' footwork, was added to the NFL Scouting Combine in 2020.

a. True

b. False

19. After his pro football career, Al Wistert became a

_____.

    a. Math teacher

    b. Life insurance salesman

    c. Realtor

    d. Electrician

20. On November 20, 2006, Andre Waters committed suicide and was subsequently diagnosed with chronic traumatic encephalopathy (CTE). Waters was portrayed by actor Richard T. Jones in the 2015 film *Concussion*.

    a. True

    b. False

QUIZ ANSWERS

1. C – Terrell Owens

2. B – False

3. D – America's Got Talent

4. B – Lay It Down: How Letting Go Brings Out Your Best

5. C – United States Army Air Forces

6. A – Troy Vincent

7. B – False

8. D – DeSean Jackson

9. A – Kobe Bryant

10. A – True

11. D – Both A and B

12. B – False

13. B – Dog fighting

14. C – Believe It: My Journey of Success, Failure, and Overcoming the Odds

15. B – Kerry Washington

16. A – True

17. D – Mike Trout

18. A – True

19. B – Life insurance salesman

20. A – True

DID YOU KNOW?

1. Terrell Owens competed on the 25th season of *Dancing with the Stars.* His partner was Cheryl Burke and he was the eighth contestant to be eliminated.

2. Herschel Walker won Season 3 of *Rachael vs. Guy: Celebrity Cook-Off,* a reality TV cooking show on the Food Network. He was a contestant in the second season of the reality television show *The Celebrity Apprentice* as well.

3. Zach Ertz is married to professional soccer player Julie Johnston, starting defensive midfielder for the U.S. women's national team and the Chicago Red Stars.

4. Jason Kelce and Beau Allen appeared in the Super Bowl LII-themed episode of *its Always Sunny in Philadelphia,* "Charlie's Home Alone."

5. At 32 years old, Sav Rocca became the oldest rookie in the history of the NFL.

6. Jeff Blake holds the record for the longest Pro Bowl touchdown run at 92 yards.

7. Rodney Peete has been married to actress Holly Robinson-Peete since 1995. He is the son of Willie Peete, former running backs coach of the Kansas City Chiefs and Chicago Bears. His brother is NFL coach Skip Peete. He is the son-in-law of late actor Matt Robinson and the cousin of the late professional golfer Calvin Peete.

8. After pro football, Ricky Watters became a motivational speaker for kids who are adopted, as he was.

9. Hank Baskett married Playboy model Kendra Wilkinson in 2009. They were co-stars on *Kendra*, a reality TV series following Wilkinson's life from 2009 to 2011. He was also on *Kendra on Top* from 2012 until 2017.

10. Herm Edwards graduated from San Diego State University with a degree in criminal justice.

CHAPTER 10:

OFFENSE

QUIZ TIME!

1. How many Pro Bowls was Terrell Owens named to during his 15-season NFL career?

    a. 2
    b. 4
    c. 6
    d. 8

2. Steve Van Buren played his entire eight-season NFL career with the Eagles.

    a. True
    b. False

3. Which of the following teams did former Eagle Michael Vick NOT play for in his 13-season NFL career?

    a. Minnesota Vikings
    b. Atlanta Falcons
    c. New York Jets
    d. Pittsburgh Steelers

4. Former Eagle Terrell Owens starred on the reality show *The Celebrity Apprentice*.

    a. True
    b. False

5. What year was Norm Van Brocklin inducted into the Pro Football Hall of Fame?

    a. 1969
    b. 1971
    c. 1973
    d. 1975

6. How many touchdowns did DeSean Jackson record during his 2009 season with the Philadelphia Eagles?

    a. 6
    b. 7
    c. 8
    d. 9

7. Pete Retzlaff played his entire 11-season NFL career with the Eagles.

    a. True
    b. False

8. Over the course of his 10-season NFL career, Ricky Watters played for the Eagles, Seattle Seahawks, and the

    _____.

    a. Arizona Cardinals
    b. San Francisco 49ers
    c. Chicago Bears
    d. Indianapolis Colts

9. How many seasons did Torrey Smith play for the Philadelphia Eagles?

    a. 1
    b. 2
    c. 3
    d. 4

10. Which of the following teams did former Eagle Herschel Walker NOT play for during his 13-season NFL career?

    a. Minnesota Vikings
    b. New York Giants
    c. Dallas Cowboys
    d. Denver Broncos

11. How many Super Bowls did Mike Ditka win in his 12-season NFL career?

    a. 0
    b. 1
    c. 2
    d. 3

12. As of the end of the 2020 season, Jason Peters has been named to nine Pro Bowls.

    a. True
    b. False

13. How many Pro Bowls has current Philadelphia Eagles quarterback Carson Wentz been named to so far (as of the end of the 2020 season)?

    a. 0
    b. 1

c. 2

d. 3

14. How many seasons did Tra Thomas play for the Philadelphia Eagles?

    a. 1

    b. 6

    c. 9

    d. 11

15. How many Super Bowl championships did Darren Sproles win in his 14-season NFL career?

    a. 1

    b. 2

    c. 3

    d. 4

16. How many Pro Bowls was Harold Carmichael named to during his 14 season NFL career?

    a. 2

    b. 3

    c. 4

    d. 5

17. What year did the Philadelphia Eagles draft Zach Ertz?

    a. 2011

    b. 2012

    c. 2013

    d. 2014

18. How many seasons did Cris Carter play for the Philadelphia Eagles?

    a. 2
    b. 3
    c. 5
    d. 7

19. How many Pro Bowls was Jerry Sisemore named to in his 12-season NFL career?

    a. 0
    b. 1
    c. 2
    d. 3

20. During his 10-season NFL career, Duce Staley played for the Philadelphia Eagles and the Pittsburgh Steelers.

    a. True
    b. False

QUIZ ANSWERS

1. C – 6

2. A – True

3. A – Minnesota Vikings

4. A – True

5. B – 1971

6. D – 9

7. A – True

8. B – San Francisco 49ers

9. A – 1

10. D – Denver Broncos

11. B – 1

12. A – True

13. B – 1

14. D – 11

15. A – 1

16. C – 4

17. C – 2013

18. B – 3

19. C – 2

20. A – True

DID YOU KNOW?

1. Current Philadelphia Eagles quarterback Carson Wentz has been with the team since 2016. He has been named to one Pro Bowl, is a one-time Super Bowl champion, and was the winner of the 2017 Bert Bell Award.

2. Michael Vick spent five years with the Philadelphia Eagles. He also played for the New York Jets, Atlanta Falcons, and Pittsburgh Steelers. He is a four-time Pro Bowler, 2010 Bert Bell Award winner, and 2010 AP Comeback Player of the Year Award winner.

3. DeSean Jackson has spent eight years with the Philadelphia Eagles. He also played for the Washington Redskins and Tampa Bay Buccaneers. So far, he has been a three-time Pro Bowler.

4. Terrell Owens spent two with the Eagles. He also played for the San Francisco 49ers, Dallas Cowboys, Buffalo Bills, and Cincinnati Bengals. He is a member of the Pro Football Hall of Fame, a six-time Pro Bowler, five-time All-Pro, and member of the HOF All-2000s Team.

5. Harold Carmichael spent 13 years with the Eagles and one year with the Dallas Cowboys. He is a member of the Pro Football Hall of Fame, a four-time Pro Bowler, 1980 Walter Payton Award Winner, and member of the HOF All-1970s Team.

6. Mike Ditka spent two years with the Eagles. He also played for the Chicago Bears and Dallas Cowboys. He is a five-time Pro Bowler, two-time All-Pro, one-time Super Bowl champion, and 1961 AP Offensive Rookie of the Year.

7. LeSean McCoy spent six years with the Philadelphia Eagles. He has also played for the Buffalo Bills, Kansas City Chiefs, and Tampa Bay Buccaneers. So far, he is a six-time Pro Bowler, two-time All-Pro, one-time Super Bowl champion, and member of the HOF All-2010s Team.

8. Herschel Walker spent three years with the Eagles. He also played for the Dallas Cowboys, Minnesota Vikings, and New York Giants. He is a two-time Pro Bowler.

9. Ron Jaworski spent 10 years with the Philadelphia Eagles. He also played for the Kansas City Chiefs, Los Angeles Rams, and Miami Dolphins. He is a one-time Pro Bowler and 1980 Bert Bell Award winner.

10. Pete Retzlaff spent his entire NFL career with the Philadelphia Eagles. He is a five-time Pro Bowler, one-time All-Pro, one-time NFL champion, and 1965 Bert Bell Award winner.

CHAPTER 11:

DEFENSE

QUIZ TIME!

1. What year was Chuck Bednarik inducted into the Pro Football Hall of Fame?

    a. 1960

    b. 1964

    c. 1967

    d. 1970

2. Jeremiah Trotter played his entire 11-season NFL career with the Philadelphia Eagles.

    a. True

    b. False

3. How many years did Andre Waters play for the Philadelphia Eagles?

    a. 6

    b. 10

    c. 11

    d. 15

4. How many Pro Bowls was Troy Vincent named to during his 16-season NFL career?

    a. 3
    b. 4
    c. 5
    d. 6

5. How many seasons did Malcolm Jenkins spend with the Philadelphia Eagles?

    a. 3
    b. 4
    c. 5
    d. 6

6. During his 12-year NFL career, Trent Cole played for the Eagles and what other team?

    a. Indianapolis Colts
    b. Cincinnati Bengals
    c. Carolina Panthers
    d. Jacksonville Jaguars

7. Brian Dawkins spent his entire 13-season NFL career with the Eagles.

    a. True
    b. False

8. How many Pro Bowls was Michael Bennett named to during his 12-season NFL career?

    a. 0
    b. 1

c. 3

d. 5

9. How many Super Bowl championships did Seth Joyner win in his 13-season NFL career?

   a. 0

   b. 1

   c. 2

   d. 3

10. How many Pro Bowls was Bill Bradley named to during his nine-year NFL career?

   a. 1

   b. 3

   c. 4

   d. 5

11. Eric Allen played for the Eagles, New Orleans Saints, and _____ during his 14-season NFL career.

   a. San Diego Chargers

   b. New England Patriots

   c. Green Bay Packers

   d. Oakland Raiders

12. Vinny Curry is the cousin of NBA star Stephen Curry.

   a. True

   b. False

13. How many Super Bowl championships did Chris Long win in his 11-season NFL career?

a. 0

b. 1

c. 2

d. 3

14. During his 11-season NFL career, Nnamdi Asomugha played for the Philadelphia Eagles, Oakland Raiders, and

_____.

    a. Houston Texans

    b. Atlanta Falcons

    c. San Francisco 49ers

    d. Arizona Cardinals

15. How many Pro Bowls was Maxie Baughan named to in his 12-season NFL career?

    a. 6

    b. 7

    c. 8

    d. 9

16. Asante Samuel played his entire 11-season NFL career with the Philadelphia Eagles.

    a. True

    b. False

17. How many seasons did Bill Bergey play for the Philadelphia Eagles?

    a. 4

    b. 5

    c. 7

    d. 9

18. What year was Richard Dent inducted into the Pro Football Hall of Fame?

    a. 2011
    b. 2012
    c. 2013
    d. 2014

19. How many Pro Bowls was Jeremiah Trotter named to during his 11-season NFL career?

    a. 2
    b. 4
    c. 6
    d. 8

20. Chuck Bednarik played his entire 14-season NFL career with the Philadelphia Eagles.

    a. True
    b. False

QUIZ ANSWERS

1. C – 1967

2. B – False (He played with the Eagles, Washington Redskins, and Tampa Bay Buccaneers.)

3. B – 10

4. C – 5

5. D – 6

6. A – Indianapolis Colts

7. B – False (He played for the Eagles and Denver Broncos.)

8. C – 3

9. B – 1

10. B – 3

11. D – Oakland Raiders

12. B – False

13. C – 2

14. C – San Francisco 49ers

15. D – 9

16. B – False (He played with the Eagles, New England Patriots, and Atlanta Falcons.)

17. C – 7

18. A – 2011

19. B – 4

20. A – True

DID YOU KNOW?

1. Chuck Bednarik spent his entire 14-season NFL career with the Philadelphia Eagles. He is a member of the Pro Football Hall of Fame, an eight-time Pro Bowler, six-time All-Pro, two-time NFL champion, and member of the Hall of Fame's All-1950s Team.

2. Jeremiah Trotter spent eight years with the Philadelphia Eagles. He also played for the Washington Redskins and Tampa Bay Buccaneers. He is a four-time Pro Bowler and one-time All-Pro

3. Troy Vincent also spent eight years with the Eagles. He also played for the Miami Dolphins, Buffalo Bills, and Washington Redskins. He is a five-time Pro Bowler, one-time All-Pro, and 2002 Walter Payton Award winner.

4. Eric Allen spent seven years with the Philadelphia Eagles. He also played for the San Francisco 49ers and Oakland Raiders. He is a six-time Pro Bowler and one-time All-Pro.

5. Maxie Baughan spent six years with the Eagles. He also played for the Los Angeles Rams and Washington Redskins. He is a nine-time Pro Bowler, two-time All-Pro, and one-time NFL champion.

6. Richard Dent spent one year with the Philadelphia Eagles. He also played for the Chicago Bears, Indianapolis Colts, and San Francisco 49ers. He is a member of the Pro

Football Hall of Fame, a four-time Pro Bowler, one-time All-Pro, and two-time Super Bowl champion.

7. Bill Bergey spent seven years with the Philadelphia Eagles. He also played for the Cincinnati Bengals. He is a five-time Pro Bowler and two-time All-Pro.

8. Seth Joyner spent eight years with the Philadelphia Eagles. He also played for the Denver Broncos, Green Bay Packers, and Arizona Cardinals. He is a three-time Pro Bowler and one-time Super Bowl champion.

9. Bill Bradley spent eight years with the Eagles. He also played for the St. Louis Cardinals. He is a three-time Pro Bowler and two-time All-Pro.

10. Trent Cole spent 10 years with the Philadelphia Eagles. He also played for the Indianapolis Colts. He is a two-time Pro Bowler.

CHAPTER 12:

SPECIAL TEAMS

QUIZ TIME!

1. How many Pro Bowls was David Akers named to during his 16-season NFL career?

    a. 1

    b. 3

    c. 6

    d. 9

2. David Akers played his entire career with the Philadelphia Eagles.

    a. True

    b. False

3. How many seasons did Norm Van Brocklin play for the Philadelphia Eagles?

    a. 3

    b. 5

    c. 7

    d. 9

4. How many Pro Bowls was Norm Van Brocklin named to during his 12-season NFL career?

    a. 1
    b. 3
    c. 6
    d. 9

5. What year was Norm Van Brocklin inducted into the Pro Football Hall of Fame?

    a. 1970
    b. 1971
    c. 1972
    d. 1973

6. How many NFL teams did former Eagle Jon Dorenbos play for during his 15-season NFL career?

    a. 2
    b. 3
    c. 4
    d. 5

7. Current Eagles long snapper Rick Lovato is the brother of singer Demi Lovato.

    a. True
    b. False

8. Former Eagles punter Donnie Jones was drafted by the _____ in the 7th round of the 2004 NFL draft.

    a. Miami Dolphins
    b. Houston Texans

c. St. Louis Rams

d. Seattle Seahawks

9. Current Eagles kicker Jake Elliott was drafted by the
_____ in the 5th round of the 2017 NFL draft.

a. Philadelphia Eagles

b. Tennessee Titans

c. Cincinnati Bengals

d. Denver Broncos

10. Current Eagles punter Cameron Johnston was born in
which country?

a. Australia

b. Canada

c. Ireland

d. Russia

11. How many Pro Bowls was Tom Dempsey named to
during his 11-season NFL career?

a. 0

b. 1

c. 2

d. 3

12. Bobby Walston played his entire 12-year NFL career with
the Philadelphia Eagles.

a. True

b. False

13. How many seasons did Roger Ruzek spend with the
Eagles?

a. 2

b. 3

c. 5

d. 7

14. In his nine-season NFL career, Horst Muhlmann played for the Philadelphia Eagles, Kansas City Chiefs, and the

_____.

a. Dallas Cowboys

b. Cleveland Browns

c. Cincinnati Bengals

d. Minnesota Vikings

15. How many Super Bowl championships did Max Runager win in his 12-season NFL career?

a. 0

b. 1

c. 2

d. 3

16. Saverio Rocca played for the Philadelphia Eagles and Washington Redskins during his seven-season NFL career.

a. True

b. False

17. How many Pro Bowls was Tony Franklin named to in his 10-season NFL career?

a. 0

b. 1

c. 2

d. 3

18. How many seasons did Alex Henery play for the Philadelphia Eagles?

    a. 1

    b. 2

    c. 3

    d. 4

19. How many Pro Bowls was Sam Baker named to during his 15-season NFL career?

    a. 2

    b. 4

    c. 5

    d. 6

20. In his six-season NFL career, Paul McFadden played for the Philadelphia Eagles, Atlanta Falcons, and New York Giants.

    a. True

    b. False

QUIZ ANSWERS

1. C – 6

2. B – False (He played for the Eagles, San Francisco 49ers, Detroit Lions, and Washington Redskins.)

3. A – 3

4. D – 9

5. B – 1971

6. B – 3 (Eagles, Buffalo Bills, and Tennessee Titans)

7. B – False

8. D – Seattle Seahawks

9. C – Cincinnati Bengals

10. A – Australia

11. B – 1

12. A – True

13. C – 5

14. C – Cincinnati Bengals

15. C – 2

16. A – True

17. B – 1

18. C – 3

19. B – 4

20. A – True

DID YOU KNOW?

1. David Akers spent 12 seasons with the Philadelphia Eagles. He is a six-time Pro Bowler, two-time All-Pro, and a member of the HOF All-2000s Team.

2. Norm Van Brocklin spent three seasons with the Eagles. He is a member of the Pro Football Hall of Fame, a nine-time Pro Bowler, one-time All-Pro, two-time NFL champion, one-time MVP, member of the HOF All-1950s Team, and 1960 Bert Bell Award winner.

3. Jon Dorenbos spent 11 seasons with the Philadelphia Eagles. He is a two-time All-Pro.

4. Rick Lovato has been with the Eagles for five seasons. He also played for the Green Bay Packers and Washington Redskins. He is a one-time Pro Bowler and one-time Super Bowl champion.

5. Donnie Jones spent five years with the Philadelphia Eagles. He also played for the St. Louis Rams, Miami Dolphins, Houston Oilers, Los Angeles Chargers, and Seattle Seahawks. He is a one-time Super Bowl champion.

6. Jake Elliott has been with the Eagles since 2017. He was drafted by the Cincinnati Bengals in 2017. He is a one-time Super Bowl champion.

7. Cameron Johnston has been with the Eagles since 2018. He was born in Geelong, Australia.

8. Tom Dempsey spent four seasons with the Philadelphia Eagles. He also played with the Buffalo Bills, New Orleans Saints, Los Angeles Rams, and Houston Oilers. He was a one-time Pro Bowler.

9. Sam Baker spent six seasons with the Eagles. He also played for the Washington Redskins, Cleveland Browns, and Dallas Cowboys. He was a four-time Pro Bowler.

10. Max Runager also spent six seasons with the Philadelphia Eagles. He also played for the San Francisco 49ers and Cleveland Browns. He was a two-time Super Bowl champion.

CHAPTER 13:

SUPER BOWL

QUIZ TIME!

1. How many Super Bowls have the Philadelphia Eagles won?

   a. 0
   b. 1
   c. 2
   d. 3

2. How many NFC championships have the Eagles won (as of the end of the 2020 season)?

   a. 3
   b. 4
   c. 6
   d. 8

3. Which team did the Philadelphia Eagles face in Super Bowl LII?

   a. Kansas City Chiefs
   b. New England Patriots

c. Denver Broncos

d. Baltimore Ravens

4. Which team did the Philadelphia Eagles face in Super Bowl XV?

   a. Cincinnati Bengals

   b. Miami Dolphins

   c. New England Patriots

   d. Oakland Raiders

5. Which team did the Philadelphia Eagles face in Super Bowl XXXIX?

   a. Pittsburgh Steelers

   b. Indianapolis Colts

   c. New England Patriots

   d. Baltimore Ravens

6. Which team did the Eagles face in the 1960 NFL Championship Game?

   a. Dallas Cowboys

   b. Cleveland Browns

   c. Chicago Bears

   d. Green Bay Packers

7. The Philadelphia Eagles have made 27 NFL playoff appearances.

   a. True

   b. False

8. Where was the 1960 NFL Championship Game played?

    a. Wrigley Field, Chicago, Illinois
    b. Yankee Stadium, New York City, New York
    c. Franklin Field, Philadelphia, Pennsylvania
    d. City Stadium, Green Bay, Wisconsin

9. Where was Super Bowl XV played?

    a. Rice Stadium, Houston, Texas
    b. Stanford Stadium, Stanford, California
    c. Louisiana Superdome, New Orleans, Louisiana
    d. Pontiac Silverdome, Pontiac, Michigan

10. Where was Super Bowl XXXIX played?

    a. Tampa Stadium, Tampa, Florida
    b. Miami Orange Bowl, Miami, Florida
    c. San Diego Jack Murphy Stadium, San Diego, California
    d. Alltel Stadium, Jacksonville, Florida

11. Where was Super Bowl LII played?

    a. Mercedes-Benz Stadium, Atlanta, Georgia
    b. U.S. Bank Stadium, Minneapolis, Minnesota
    c. Hard Rock Stadium, Miami Gardens, Florida
    d. Levi's Stadium, Santa Clara, California

12. Doug Pederson was head coach of the Philadelphia Eagles when they won Super Bowl LII.

    a. True
    b. False

13. Who was head coach of the Eagles when they played in Super Bowl XXXIX?

   a. Chip Kelly
   b. Andy Reid
   c. Doug Pederson
   d. Ray Rhodes

14. Who was head coach of the Eagles when they won the 1960 NFL Championship Game?

   a. Jim Trimble
   b. Dick Vermeil
   c. Buck Shaw
   d. Nick Skorich

15. Who played the halftime show at Super Bowl LII?

   a. Lady Gaga
   b. Justin Timberlake
   c. Maroon 5
   d. Bruno Mars

16. Pink sang the National Anthem before Super Bowl LII.

   a. True
   b. False

17. Which former Eagles player was named the MVP of Super Bowl LII?

   a. Zach Ertz
   b. Carson Wentz
   c. Nick Foles
   d. Darren Sproles

18. Who played the halftime show at Super Bowl XXXIX?

    a. U2

    b. Prince

    c. The Rolling Stones

    d. Paul McCartney

19. The Eagles winning Super Bowl LII ended the third-longest active NFL championship drought at _____ years.

    a. 37

    b. 47

    c. 57

    d. 67

20. Super Bowl LII set a Super Bowl record for fewest punts by both teams.

    a. True

    b. False

QUIZ ANSWERS

1. B – 1 (2017)

2. A – 3 (1980, 2004, 2017)

3. B – New England Patriots

4. D – Oakland Raiders

5. C – New England Patriots

6. D – Green Bay Packers

7. A – True

8. C – Franklin Field, Philadelphia, Pennsylvania

9. C – Louisiana Superdome, New Orleans, Louisiana

10. D – Alltel Stadium, Jacksonville, Florida

11. B – U.S. Bank Stadium, Minneapolis, Minnesota

12. A – True

13. B – Andy Reid

14. C – Buck Shaw

15. B – Justin Timberlake

16. A – True

17. C – Nick Foles

18. D – Paul McCartney

19. C – 57

20. A – True

DID YOU KNOW?

1. The final score of the 1960 NFL Championship Game was Eagles 17, Packers 13.

2. Super Bowl XV had a final score of Raiders 27, Eagles 10.

3. In Super Bowl XXXIX, the Patriots beat the Eagles, 24 to 21.

4. Super Bowl LII had a final score of Eagles 41, Patriots 33.

5. Super Bowl LII was only the second time that a Super Bowl was played in Minneapolis, the northernmost city ever to host the Super Bowl.

6. Nick Foles, who completed 28 of 43 pass attempts for 373 yards and 3 touchdowns with 1 interception and also caught a 1-yard touchdown pass on a trick play, was named Super Bowl LII MVP. Foles's touchdown catch later became known as the "Philly Special."

7. The broadcast of Super Bowl LII on NBC had the smallest Super Bowl audience in nine years, with an average of 103.4 million viewers.

8. Super Bowl LII set a record for most yards gained in an NFL game by both teams combined (1,151).

9. Super Bowl LII marked the fourth time in five years that the Super Bowl had featured the top team from each conference.

10. The cost of a 30-second commercial during Super Bowl LII was $5 million.

CHAPTER 14:

HEATED RIVALRIES

QUIZ TIME!

1. Which team does NOT play in the NFC East with the Philadelphia Eagles?

    a. New York Giants

    b. Washington Football Team

    c. Buffalo Bills

    d. Dallas Cowboys

2. The "Bounty Bowl" was the name given to two NFL games held in 1989 between the Philadelphia Eagles and Dallas Cowboys. The first, a Thanksgiving Day game in Dallas, was noted for allegations that the Eagles put a $200 bounty on Cowboys kicker Luis Zendejas, who had been cut by Philadelphia earlier that season. The second was a rematch held two weeks later in Philadelphia. The Eagles were favored to win both games and they did.

    a. True

    b. False

3. The Eagles have one Super Bowl championship. How many do the Dallas Cowboys have?

    a. 1
    b. 3
    c. 5
    d. 7

4. The Eagles have one Super Bowl championship. How many does the Washington Football Team have?

    a. 1
    b. 2
    c. 3
    d. 4

5. The Eagles have one Super Bowl championship. How many do the New York Giants have?

    a. 0
    b. 1
    c. 2
    d. 4

6. The Eagles have one Super Bowl championship. How many do the Pittsburgh Steelers have?

    a. 8
    b. 6
    c. 4
    d. 2

7. The Philadelphia Eagles have the most NFC East championships of any team in the division.

a. True

b. False

8. The Arizona Cardinals were members of the NFC East alongside the Eagles from 1970 to 2001.

   a. True

   b. False

9. The Eagles and New York Giants have played in the same division in the NFL every year since _____.

   a. 1923

   b. 1933

   c. 1943

   d. 1953

10. As of the end of the 2020 season, how many Super Bowl championships have been won by NFC East teams?

    a. 10

    b. 11

    c. 13

    d. 15

11. The very first game between the Eagles and Dallas Cowboys took place in _____.

    a. 1960

    b. 1965

    c. 1970

    d. 1975

12. The Eagles-Cowboys rivalry was ranked number one overall in the NFL in 1992 and 2014.

a. True

b. False

13. What is a game between the Eagles and Pittsburgh Steelers referred to as?

    a. The Steagles Series

    b. The Pennsylvania Series

    c. The Liberty Bell Series

    d. The Battle of Pennsylvania

14. As of the end of the 2020 season, how many times have the Eagles and Dallas Cowboys met in the playoffs?

    a. 0

    b. 1

    c. 2

    d. 4

15. As of the end of the 2020 season, how many times have the Eagles and New York Giants met in the playoffs?

    a. 0

    b. 1

    c. 2

    d. 4

16. The Eagles have never faced the Washington Football Team in the playoffs.

    a. True

    b. False

17. As of the end of the 2020 season, how many times have the Eagles and Pittsburgh Steelers met in the playoffs?

a. 0

b. 1

c. 2

d. 3

18. The NFC East was formed in 1967 as the _____.

  a. NFC Capital East Division

  b. NFL Eastern Capitol Division

  c. National Football League Capitol Division

  d. National Football Capital Division

19. Because the NFC East teams are in some of the United States' largest media markets, the NFC East receives a high amount of coverage from national sports media outlets.

  a. True

  b. False

20. The Philadelphia Eagles have the most playoff berths of any team in the NFC East.

  a. True

  b. False

QUIZ ANSWERS

1. C – Buffalo Bills

2. A – True

3. C – 5

4. C – 3

5. D – 4

6. B – 6

7. B – False (This milestone belongs to the Dallas Cowboys.)

8. A – True

9. B – 1933

10. C – 13

11. A – 1960

12. A – True

13. D – The Battle of Pennsylvania

14. D – 4

15. D – 4

16. B – False (once)

17. B – 1

18. C – National Football League Capitol Division

19. A – True

20. B – False (This milestone belongs to the Dallas Cowboys.)

DID YOU KNOW?

1. The Dallas Cowboys have the most NFC East division championships with 23. The Eagles are second with 11. The Washington Football Team has 9, the New York Giants have 8, and the Arizona Cardinals (who are no longer in the NFC East) have 2.

2. *Sports Illustrated* ranks the Eagles-Giants rivalry as the fourth best NFL rivalry of all time.

3. The NFC East is currently the only division in the NFL in which all four teams have won at least one Super Bowl championship.

4. At the time of this writing, the Dallas Cowboys lead the all-time series with the Eagles by 69-54-0.

5. At the time of this writing, the Eagles lead the all-time series with the New York Giants by 89-87-2.

6. At the time of this writing, the Washington Football Team leads the all-time series with the Eagles by 87-80-6.

7. At the time of this writing, the Eagles lead the all-time series with the Pittsburgh Steelers by 48-29-3.

8. The NFC East teams have combined to be the most successful division in the NFL since the 1970 NFL merger. Collectively, they have 21 NFC championship wins and 13 Super Bowl victories, the most of any division in the NFL.

9. The Philadelphia Eagles are the only NFC East team to actually play in the city of the team's naming, Philadelphia. The Dallas Cowboys play in Arlington, Texas; the Washington Football Team plays in Landover, Maryland; and the New York Giants play in East Rutherford, New Jersey.

10. There have been no repeat NFC East division winners in 15 years. This is the longest current NFC East and NFL streak.

CHAPTER 15:

THE AWARDS SECTION

QUIZ TIME!

1. Which former Eagle won the Bart Starr Award in 1992?

    a. Herschel Walker

    b. Randall Cunningham

    c. Reggie White

    d. Eric Allen

2. LeScan McCoy was named the 2007 Big East Rookie of the Year.

    a. True

    b. False

3. Which Eagles player won the Bert Bell Award in 2017?

    a. Nick Foles

    b. Carson Wentz

    c. Torrey Smith

    d. Zach Ertz

4. Norm Van Brocklin was named NFL MVP and the Bert Bell Award winner in _____.

a. 1958

b. 1959

c. 1960

d. He was never awarded either of these honors.

5. When did Troy Vincent win the Walter Payton Man of the Year Award and the Whizzer White NFL Man of the Year Award?

a. 2000

b. 2001

c. 2002

d. 2003

6. Which Eagles player was named the NFC Player of the Year in 1980?

a. Ron Jaworski

b. Harold Carmichael

c. Wilbert Montgomery

d. Randy Logan

7. DeSean Jackson won the Glenn Davis Award in 2004. The award is given annually by the *Los Angeles Times* to the best high school player in the L.A. area.

a. True

b. False

8. Michael Vick won the Bert Bell Award and was named the NFL Comeback Player of the Year in _____.

a. 2009

b. 2010

c. 2011

d. 2012

9. When did Herschel Walker win the Heisman Trophy?

 a. 1979

 b. 1980

 c. 1981

 d. 1982

10. Andy Reid was named the AP NFL Coach of the Year in
 _____.

 a. 2002

 b. 2005

 c. 2007

 d. 2012

11. When was Doug Pederson named the Maxwell Club's NFL Coach of the Year?

 a. 2016

 b. 2017

 c. 2018

 d. 2019

12. Pete Retzlaff received the Bert Bell Award in 1965.

 a. True

 b. False

13. When did the Eagles' offensive line win the Built Ford Tough Offensive Line of the Year Award?

 a. 2013

 b. 2015

c. 2017

d. 2019

14. Which former Eagle won the ESPN ESPY Award for Best Championship Performance in 2018?

a. Zach Ertz

b. Darren Sproles

c. Carson Wentz

d. Nick Foles

15. Jalen Hurts won a Big 12 championship in _____ with the Oklahoma Sooners.

a. 2016

b. 2017

c. 2018

d. 2019

16. Rodney Peete won the Heisman Trophy in 1988.

a. True

b. False

17. Brian Westbrook was named the winner of the Walter Payton Award in _____.

a. 1998

b. 1999

c. 2000

d. 2001

18. When was LeSean McCoy named the Big East Offensive Player of the Year?

a. 2007

b. 2008

c. 2009

d. 2010

19. Which of the following celebrities has NOT hosted the NFL Honors Awards Show (as of the 2020 season)?

a. Alec Baldwin

b. Steve Harvey

c. Seth Meyers

d. Jimmy Fallon

20. David Akers won a PFW Golden Toe Award in 2011.

a. True

b. False

QUIZ ANSWERS

1. C – Reggie White

2. A – True

3. B – Carson Wentz

4. C – 1960

5. C – 2002

6. A – Ron Jaworski

7. A – True

8. B – 2010

9. D – 1982

10. A – 2002

11. B – 2017

12. A – True

13. C – 2017

14. D – Nick Foles

15. D – 2019

16. B – False (Peete was a runner-up.)

17. D – 2001

18. B – 2008

19. D – Jimmy Fallon

20. A – True

DID YOU KNOW?

1. Troy Vincent won the Bart Starr Award in 2005.

2. Ron Jaworski won the Bert Bell Award in 1980.

3. Zach Ertz was a Pac-12 champion in 2012 with Stanford University.

4. The NFL hosts an NFL honors show each year to give out awards such as MVP, Rookie of the Year, and Coach of the Year. NFL Honors debuted in Indianapolis in 2012. It is hosted in the city that is hosting the Super Bowl on the network that is carrying that year's championship game.

5. Caleb Sturgis was named the SEC Special Teams Player of the Year in 2012.

6. Randall Cunningham is a three-time Bert Bell Award winner (1988, 1990, and 1998). He was also named the NFL Comeback Player of the Year in 1992 and the NFL MVP in 1990 and 1998.

7. Carson Wentz was named the NFC Offensive Player of the Week for Week 3 in 2016 and Week 7 in 2017.

8. Donovan McNabb was named the NFC Offensive Player of the Month in September 2002, November 2003, September 2004, and September 2005.

9. Reggie White was named the NFC Defensive Player of the Month in December 1988 and September 1998.

10. Brian Dawkins was named the NFC Defensive Player of the Month in December 2006 and December 2008.

CHAPTER 16:

THE CITY OF BROTHERLY LOVE

QUIZ TIME!

1. What was the Liberty Bell originally called?

    a. American Bell

    b. State House Bell

    c. USA Bell

    d. Philly Bell

2. The Walnut Street Theater was originally owned by Edwin Booth, John Wilkes Booth's brother.

    a. True

    b. False

3. Philly is known as the _____ capital of the United States.

    a. Agriculture

    b. Technology

    c. Sandwich

    d. Mural

4. People in Philadelphia consume ___ times more pretzels annually than the average American.

    a. 4

    b. 8

    c. 12

    d. 16

5. What percent of America's population lives within five hours of Philadelphia? Over what percent of Americans live within a two-hour flight to Philadelphia?

    a. 5, 10

    b. 10, 30

    c. 20, 40

    d. 25, 60

6. Eastern State Penitentiary in Philadelphia once held which famous criminal?

    a. Al Capone

    b. "Slick Willie" Sutton

    c. Morris "The Rabbi" Bolber

    d. All of the above

7. On the Liberty Bell, Pennsylvania is spelled with only one "N."

    a. True

    b. False

8. Which famous actor is from the City of Brotherly Love?

    a. Johnny Depp

    b. Tom Hanks

c. Will Smith

d. Robert Downey Jr.

9. What is the name of Philadelphia's MLB team?

   a. Philadelphia Phillies

   b. Philadelphia Pirates

   c. Philadelphia Cardinals

   d. Philadelphia Penguins

10. What is the name of Philadelphia's NBA team?

    a. Philadelphia Heat

    b. Philadelphia Warriors

    c. Philadelphia Magic

    d. Philadelphia 76ers

11. What is the name of Philadelphia's NHL team?

    a. Philadelphia Kings

    b. Philadelphia Penguins

    c. Philadelphia Flyers

    d. Philadelphia Lightning

12. Philadelphia's MLS team is called the Philadelphia Union.

    a. True

    b. False

13. Where in Philadelphia were the Declaration of Independence and the Constitution signed?

    a. Philadelphia City Hall

    b. Christ Church

    c. Independence Hall

    d. One Liberty Place

14. What building's steps were immortalized in the run-up the stairs scene in the film *Rocky*?

    a. Philadelphia Museum of Art
    b. Independence Hall
    c. The Franklin Institute
    d. Rodin Museum

15. What is the name of the arena where the Philadelphia 76ers of the NBA and the Philadelphia Flyers of the NHL play?

    a. Pepsi Center
    b. Wells Fargo Center
    c. United Center
    d. Smoothie King Center

16. What is the name of the stadium where the Philadelphia Phillies play?

    a. Fenway Park
    b. Citizens Bank Park
    c. PNC Park
    d. Petco Park

17. Which famous basketball player was born in Philadelphia?

    a. LeBron James
    b. Kobe Bryant
    c. Steph Curry
    d. Shaquille O'Neal

18. What is Philadelphia International Airport's code?

    a. PHD
    b. PIA

c. PIL

d. PHL

19. One out of every ____ doctors in the United States was trained in Philadelphia.

    a. 3

    b. 6

    c. 8

    d. 10

20. Central High School in Philadelphia is the only high school in America that can grant bachelor's degrees to its students.

    a. True

    b. False

QUIZ ANSWERS

1. B – State House Bell

2. A – True

3. D – Mural

4. C – 12

5. D – 25, 60

6. D – All of the above

7. A – True

8. C – Will Smith

9. A – Philadelphia Phillies

10. D – Philadelphia 76ers

11. C – Philadelphia Flyers

12. A – True

13. C – Independence Hall

14. A – Philadelphia Museum of Art

15. B – Wells Fargo Center

16. B – Citizens Bank Park

17. B – Kobe Bryant

18. D – PHL

19. B – 6

20. A – True

DID YOU KNOW?

1. Philadelphia was home to the first hospital, medical school, zoo, newspaper, soft pretzel, lager beer, cheesesteak sandwich, lending library, fire company, naval shipyard in America, mint in America, and general use computer.

2. The first Republican National Convention was held at Philadelphia's Musical Fund Hall in June 1856.

3. Bartram's Garden is the oldest botanical garden in North America. The Penn Museum is home to the largest Egyptian Sphynx in the Western Hemisphere.

4. The Mütter Museum is home to several oddities, including slices of Albert Einstein's brain, tissue from the body of John Wilkes Booth, a corpse that turned into soap, and a tumor removed from President Grover Cleveland.

5. In an April Fool's Day prank in 1996, Taco Bell took out a full-page ad in six major newspapers claiming they had purchased the Liberty Bell and renamed it the "Taco Liberty Bell." People were outraged, to say the least. April Fool's!

6. "In West Philadelphia born and raised/On the playground is where I spent most of my days/Chilling out, maxing, relaxing all cool and all shooting some b-ball outside of the school/When a couple of guys who were up to no good started making trouble in my neighborhood/I got in one

little fight and my mom got scared/And said, 'You're moving with your auntie and uncle in Bel-Air.'" – Lyrics to *The Fresh Prince of Bel-Air* theme song

7. The famous Philly Cheesesteak was created in 1930 by Pat Olivieri, who owned a hot dog stand. According to his grand-nephew, the current owner of Pat's King of Steaks, it originally did not have cheese on it. It was originally steak and onions on a hot dog bun. The provolone cheese was added a little over a decade later.

8. About 50 tree seedlings traveled to space with the Apollo 14 mission. One of these "moon trees" was planted in Philly's Washington Square Park. When the tree began to die in 2011, the National Park Service replaced it with a clone.

9. Philadelphia is home to more impressionist paintings than any other city in the world except Paris. Philly also has a Rodin Museum, which makes the city the largest collector of the sculptor's work outside of Paris.

10. Of the 100 questions on the United States Citizenship Test, half of the answers can be found in Philadelphia. The city is like one huge American history lesson.

CHAPTER 17:

FIVE

QUIZ TIME!

1. Where was Donovan McNabb born?

    a. Detroit, Michigan

    b. Chicago, Illinois

    c. Oakland, California

    d. Phoenix, Arizona

2. Donovan McNabb played his entire career with the Philadelphia Eagles.

    a. True

    b. False

3. Where did Donovan McNabb attend college?

    a. Texas A&M University

    b. Syracuse University

    c. University of Michigan

    d. University of Georgia

4. How many seasons did Donovan McNabb spend with the Philadelphia Eagles?

a. 8

b. 10

c. 11

d. 13

5. What year was Donovan McNabb drafted by the Philadelphia Eagles in the 1st round (2nd overall)?

a. 1997

b. 1999

c. 2001

d. 2003

6. How many Super Bowls did Donovan McNabb win?

a. 0

b. 1

c. 2

d. 3

7. Donovan McNabb was named the Big East Offensive Player of the Decade for the 1990s.

a. True

b. False

8. How many Pro Bowls was Donovan McNabb named to?

a. 1

b. 3

c. 5

d. 6

9. What year was Donovan McNabb inducted into the Philadelphia Eagles Hall of Fame?

a. 2011

b. 2012

c. 2013

d. 2014

10. Donovan McNabb and his mom, Wilma, did popular commercials together for _____.

a. Bush's Baked Beans

b. Target

c. Coca-Cola

d. Campbell's Chunky Soup

11. When was Donovan McNabb named the Big East Rookie of the Year?

a. 1993

b. 1995

c. 1997

d. 1998

12. Donovan McNabb was the first NFL quarterback to throw for more than 30 touchdowns and fewer than 10 interceptions in a season (2004).

a. True

b. False

13. Donovan McNabb has a Bachelor of Science degree in _____ from Syracuse University.

a. Biology

b. Sports medicine

c. Cognitive science

d. Speech communication

14. What number did Donovan McNabb wear as a member of the Philadelphia Eagles?

    a. 5
    b. 15
    c. 25
    d. 55

15. What age was Donovan McNabb when he made his NFL debut?

    a. 21
    b. 22
    c. 23
    d. 24

16. Donovan McNabb was the fourth quarterback in NFL history to collect more than 30,000 passing yards, 200 touchdown passes, 3,000 rushing yards, and 20 rushing touchdowns in his career.

    a. True
    b. False

17. Donovan McNabb is tied with Jim Kelly for the most playoff wins by a quarterback who did not win a Super Bowl, with _____.

    a. 7
    b. 8
    c. 9
    d. 11

18. Donovan McNabb's niece Kia Nurse is a professional basketball player in the WNBA. She currently plays for the _____.

    a. Chicago Sky

    b. New York Liberty

    c. Sacramento Monarchs

    d. Los Angeles Sparks

19. What other sport did Donovan McNabb play at Syracuse University besides football?

    a. Baseball

    b. Track & field

    c. Soccer

    d. Basketball

20. Donovan McNabb is the Philadelphia Eagles' all-time leader in pass attempts, pass completions, passing yards, and passing touchdowns.

    a. True

    b. False

QUIZ ANSWERS

1. B – Chicago, Illinois

2. B – False (He played with the Eagles, Washington Redskins, and Minnesota Vikings.)

3. B – Syracuse University

4. C – 11

5. B – 1999

6. A – 0

7. A – True

8. D – 6

9. C – 2013

10. D – Campbell's Chunky Soup

11. B – 1995

12. A – True

13. D – Speech communication

14. A – 5

15. C – 23

16. A – True

17. C – 9

18. B – New York Liberty

19. D – Basketball

20. A – True

DID YOU KNOW?

1. Donovan McNabb's nephew Darnell Nurse plays for the Edmonton Oilers. His niece Sarah Nurse competed on Team Canada's National Women's Hockey Team at the 2018 Winter Olympics. I think it's safe to say sports are a hot topic at family get-togethers.

2. Donovan McNabb's No. 5 has been retired by both the Philadelphia Eagles and Syracuse University football.

3. Donovan McNabb was the Philadelphia Eagles' starting quarterback from 1999 to 2009. During his time in Philly, he led the Eagles to eight NFL playoff appearances.

4. In high school, Donovan McNabb played on his high school's basketball team alongside former NBA player Antoine Walker. In high school, McNabb also competed in track and field.

5. Donovan McNabb led the NFL in quarterback wins from 2000 to 2004.

6. Donovan McNabb married his college sweetheart Raquel Ann Sarah "Roxie" Nurse in June of 2003.

7. Donovan McNabb was named to Syracuse University's board of trustees. He is one of the youngest trustees to have served on the board.

8. In October of 2007, Donovan McNabb wrote a song for Adrian College that debuted in a game against Olivet College.

9. Donovan McNabb was named to the Philadelphia Eagles 75th Anniversary Team.

10. On July 29, 2013, Donovan McNabb officially retired from the NFL as a member of the Philadelphia Eagles.

CHAPTER 18:

WEAPON X

QUIZ TIME!

1. Where was Brian Dawkins born?

    a. San Diego, California

    b. Tucson, Arizona

    c. Jacksonville, Florida

    d. Scranton, Pennsylvania

2. Brian Dawkins played his entire NFL career with the Philadelphia Eagles.

    a. True

    b. False

3. Where did Brian Dawkins attend college?

    a. Auburn University

    b. Vanderbilt University

    c. University of Notre Dame

    d. Clemson University

4. Brian Dawkins was the first player in NFL history to record a sack, an interception, forced fumble, and touchdown reception in a single game.

    a. True
    b. False

5. How many Pro Bowls was Brian Dawkins named to?

    a. 5
    b. 9
    c. 10
    d. 12

6. How many Super Bowl championships did Brian Dawkins win?

    a. 0
    b. 1
    c. 3
    d. 4

7. Brian Dawkins was nicknamed "Weapon X" after the codename of the Marvel Comics character Wolverine due to his reputation for relentless aggression.

    a. True
    b. False

8. In addition to his playing career, Brian Dawkins served as the Eagles' executive of football operations for player development from 2016 to _____ and was with the organization when they won Super Bowl LII.

    a. 2017
    b. 2018

c. 2019

d. He is still currently in that role.

9. How many times was Brian Dawkins named a First-Team All-Pro?

   a. 1

   b. 2

   c. 3

   d. 4

10. Brian Dawkins was drafted in the 2nd round (61st overall) in the _____ NFL draft by the Philadelphia Eagles.

    a. 1995

    b. 1996

    c. 1997

    d. 1998

11. When was Brian Dawkins inducted into the Pro Football Hall of Fame?

    a. 2016

    b. 2017

    c. 2018

    d. 2019

12. On January 11, 2013, Clemson University established the Brian Dawkins Lifetime Achievement Award to annually honor a former Clemson player for his performance on the field, contributions in leadership, and community service.

    a. True

    b. False

13. How many times was Brian Dawkins named a Second-Team All-Pro?

    a. 0
    b. 1
    c. 2
    d. 3

14. Brian Dawkins was named the Whizzer White NFL Man of the Year in _____.

    a. 2004
    b. 2005
    c. 2007
    d. 2008

15. Brian Dawkins was the first player in NFL history to record at least ____ interceptions and ____ forced fumbles in a career.

    a. 15
    b. 25
    c. 30
    d. 35

16. Brian Dawkins's No. 20 is retired by the Philadelphia Eagles.

    a. True
    b. False

17. How many seasons did Brian Dawkins play for the Philadelphia Eagles?

    a. 10
    b. 11

c. 13

d. 15

18. Brian Dawkins is the only player in NFL history with 25+ interceptions, forced fumbles, and sacks.

a. True

b. False

19. When was Brian Dawkins inducted into Clemson University's Athletic Hall of Fame?

a. 2007

b. 2009

c. 2010

d. 2012

20. Brian Dawkins is a member of the NFL 20/20 Club.

a. True

b. False

QUIZ ANSWERS

1. C – Jacksonville, Florida

2. B – False (He played for the Eagles and Denver Broncos.)

3. D – Clemson University

4. A – True

5. B – 9

6. A – 0

7. A – True

8. B – 2018

9. D – 4

10. B – 1996

11. C – 2018

12. A – True

13. B – 1

14. D – 2008

15. C – 30

16. A – True

17. C – 13

18. A – True

19. B – 2009

20. A – True

DID YOU KNOW?

1. In April 2019, Wawa and Brian Dawkins collaborated to create a hoagie called "The Dawk." It had grilled chicken, Parmesan cheese, spinach, tomato, pickles, sweet peppers, and yellow mustard. It was available for a limited time and only at the Wawa in Dawkins's hometown of Jacksonville, Florida.

2. Brian Dawkins's nephew Dalyn Dawkins played for Colorado State and is currently with the Tennessee Titans.

3. Brian Dawkins forced 36 fumbles in his NFL career, the most ever by an NFL safety.

4. Brian Dawkins was named to the HOF All-2000s Team.

5. Brian Dawkins was named to the Philadelphia Eagles 75th Anniversary Team.

6. Brian Dawkins was named the first-team strong safety on Clemson's all-centennial team in 1996.

7. Brian Dawkins attended William M. Raines High School in Jacksonville, Florida.

8. Brian Dawkins spent the final three seasons of his NFL career with the Denver Broncos, from 2009 to 2011.

9. In 2012, Brian Dawkins was hired as an NFL studio analyst by ESPN.

10. Brian Dawkins has said that his Christian faith has helped against depression and suicidal thoughts.

CONCLUSION

Learn anything new? Now you truly are the ultimate Eagles fan! Not only did you learn about the Eagles of the modern era, but you also expanded your knowledge about the early days of the franchise.

You learned about the Eagles' origins and their history. You learned about the history of their uniforms and jersey numbers. You identified some famous quotes and read some of the craziest nicknames of all time. You learned more about star quarterback Donovan McNabb and the legendary Reggie White and Brian Dawkins. You were amazed by Eagles stats and recalled some of the most famous Eagles trades and draft picks of all time. You broke down your knowledge by offense, defense, and special teams. You looked back on the Eagles' championships and playoff feats and the awards that came before, after, and during them. You also learned about the Eagles' fiercest rivalries inside and outside of their division.

Every team in the NFL has a storied history, but the Eagles have one of the most memorable of all. They have won one treasured Lombard Trophy with the backing of their devoted fans. Being the ultimate Eagles fan takes knowledge and a whole lot of patience, which you tested with this book.

Whether you knew every answer or were stumped by several questions, you learned some of the most baffling history that the game of football has to offer.

The deep history of the Eagles franchise represents what we all love about the game of football; the heart, the determination, the tough times, and the unexpected moments. The players that inspire and encourage us to do our best, because even if you get knocked down, there is always another game and another (Sun)day.

With players like Jalen Hurts, Zach Ertz, and DeSean Jackson, the future for the Eagles continues to look bright. They have a lot to prove but there is no doubt that this franchise will continue to be one of the most competitive teams in the NFL year after year.

It's a new decade, which means there is a clean slate, ready to continue writing the history of the Philadelphia Eagles. The ultimate Eagles fan cannot wait to see what's to come for their beloved Birds. Fly, Eagles, Fly!